THE RIGHT ROAD
TO PONTYPOOL

The Right Road to Pontypool

Alex Poch-Goldin

The Right Road to Pontypool
first published 2018 by Scirocco Drama
An imprint of J. Gordon Shillingford Publishing Inc.

Scirocco Drama Editor: Glenda MacFarlane

Cover design by Terry Gallagher/Doowah Design

Cover image: Three boys of Pontypool, [ca. 1934].
Ontario Jewish Archives, Blankenstein Family Heritage Centre.

Author photo by Tim Leyes
Production photos by Wayne Eardley – Brookside Studios

Printed and bound in Canada on 100% post-consumer recycled paper.
We acknowledge the financial support of the Manitoba Arts Council and
The Canada Council for the Arts for our publishing program.

Production inquiries should be addressed to:
Ian Arnold: ian@catalysttcm.com
#312 – 100 Broadview Ave. Toronto, ON, Canada M4M 3H3

Library and Archives Canada Cataloguing in Publication

Library and Archives Canada Cataloguing in Publication

Poch-Goldin, Alex, author
The right road to Pontypool / Alex Poch-Goldin. -- First edition.

A play.
ISBN 978-1-927922-45-3 (softcover)

I. Title.

PS8581.O15R54 2018 C812'.6 C2018-904469-1

J. Gordon Shillingford Publishing
P.O. Box 86, RPO Corydon Avenue, Winnipeg, MB Canada R3M 3S3

For my parents and my brother, Sam.

My family flows through me like a river.

Alex Poch-Goldin

Alex Poch-Goldin is an award-winning playwright and librettist. His work has been produced internationally and across Canada. He has developed and produced work at Canadian Stage, Tarragon Theatre, Factory Theatre, Theatre Passe Muraille, Buddies in Bad Times Theatre, 4th Line Theatre, Winnipeg Jewish Theatre, Citadel Compagnie, and others. His plays include: *Yahrzeit* (Toronto Jewish Playwriting Award / German national tour); *The Right Road to Pontypool/The Bad Luck Bank Robbers/The Great Shadow* (4th Line); *The Life of Jude* (Summerworks); *Jim and Shorty* (Factory), and *Internazionale*. His plays *Cringeworthy* and *This Hotel* were both nominated for Dora Awards for Outstanding New Play. Alex's plays have been translated into both German and French.

Alex has also created several dance / opera theatricals including acclaimed adaptations of *The House of Mirth* and *Against Nature*. Alex's full-length opera *The Shadow* was produced to great success by Tapestry New Opera. He has developed projects for CBC Radio, Bravo! Television and was a nominee for the Siminovitch Prize for Playwriting. Alex is also an award-winning actor and has worked extensively in theatre, film, radio, and television. He is a graduate of The Dome Theatre in Montreal and the National Theatre Institute in Connecticut.

He lives in Toronto with his delightful daughter, Chloe Babette.

Acknowledgements

I am indebted to Grant Curtis for the insight and research he conducted for his book *Laugh and the World Laughs with You, in Pontypool,* which was the source of much information for this play; to Doris Manetta, who was a tireless liaison for me into the world that existed and the people who shaped it; to Robert Winslow for conceiving of the project and entrusting it to me; and to the indomitable Kim Blackwell for her skill, passion, and collaborative spirit that so movingly and lovingly brought Pontypool to life. I also would like to thank the myriad of actors who workshopped this play and helped it to find its legs, particularly Paul Soles and Theresa Tova.

I am grateful to the Canada Council for the Arts, the Ontario Arts Council, the Toronto Arts Council, and 4th Line Theatre for their support in the creation of this work.

Foreword

By Richard Greenblatt

I had the unmitigated pleasure of acting in the remount of Alex Poch-Goldin's play *The Right Road to Pontypool* at 4th Line Theatre in the summer of 2010. As soon as we opened, I could see why it had worked so well the previous year. The play connects to its audience in an immediate, visceral way. It deals with many issues and theatrical devices concurrently, combining comedy, historical documentary, social commentary, nostalgia, issues of cultural loss, and plain old human personal dilemmas, all wrapped up in an engaging and fast-paced story.

But the strongest element for me was its geographical specificity. 4th Line is one of a few Canadian theatres (the Blyth Festival and the Caravan Stage Company also spring to mind) that commissions narratives about its environs, elevating local stories to epic sagas worthy of wide public consumption. This tale about nearby summer resorts for working-class Jews – from its inception to its disappearance – connects to anyone who witnesses it, precisely because of its specific nature. There were quite a few people who saw the show that had spent many summers in the resorts in and around Pontypool, and unsurprisingly, it was a powerful and moving experience for them. But equally fascinating to me were the thousands of others who had no connection to the place or its history whatsoever, and who seemed equally moved. It serves to remind us all that to communicate to the many, you must start by communicating with as much honesty, truth, and especially specificity about your own story as you possibly can.

The play is really an unselfconscious allegory for many issues: xenophobia, class struggle, and assimilation, amongst others. As a Jew, I am only one generation removed from overt anti-Semitism ("No Dogs or Jews Allowed" read the sign at Sunnyside Pool in

Toronto right up until the 1940s), and the immigration quotas imposed by our government, even in the face of rising Nazism in Germany. This was the context of the creation of Pontypool's community, who were looking for a relatively safe haven, even in Protestant Ontario. And now, here we are in the Trump era, where fear and mistrust of the Other has taken root yet again. The focus of Trump and his base's hatred has transferred to Muslims, Latin Americans, African Americans, and "liberals," illustrating just how that most ugly of human instincts has not yet been purged from our DNA.

Alex's play is an antidote to such cynicism and hatred. Its themes of acceptance and inclusiveness, without sappiness or sugar-coated solutions, remind us all of our better natures. It pays homage to the past with a nod to the future, knowing that to forget our history will not only doom us to repeat its mistakes, but would also impoverish us all. It reminds us that out of human suffering and hardship can come great beauty, generosity, and even humour.

These themes are the reasons that I am an artist, and why I loved performing in this play.

Richard Greenblatt is an actor, director, playwright, and musician who has been working in the theatre in Canada and abroad for over forty-three years, and is still in love with the art form.

Production History

The Right Road to Pontypool was commissioned and produced by 4th Line Theatre at their beautiful outdoor theatre in Millbrook, Ontario in 2009/10. It was directed by Kim Blackwell with the following cast:

Elly-Ray Hennessy .... Doris (Narrator)

Richard Greenblatt/Allan Price .... Harold (Narrator)

Caitlin Driscoll .... Young Doris

Dov Mickelson .... Moishe Yukle Bernstein (and others)

Peter Pasyk .... Zev (and others)

Robert Winslow .... Zev (2010)

Griffin Clark .... Young Harold

The ensemble included: Mark Hiscox, Matt Gilbert, Marsala Lukianchuk/Leora Morris, Justin Hiscox, Jordan Kanner, Marie Jones, Bridget Norris, Gerry Gray, Luke Foster, Graeme Browning, Stewart Hanmore, Dan Ladoucier, Ray Barker, Lauren Murphy, Anika Spasov, Emilie Spasov, Peter Spasov, Renata Spasov, Maura Wingle-Land, Shawna Blackwood, Lee Oliver, Anne Lukaszewicz, Annie Gleason, Christina Adams, Linda Driscoll, Cody McMahon, Françoise Bouchard, Meg O'Sullivan, Laura Cournoyea, Whitney Wakefield, and Craig Dawson.

Costume Design: Anne Redish
Set Design: Elizabeth Nutting
Stage Manager: Laura Cournoyea
Music Direction: Justin Hiscox

Cast of Characters

MOISHE Yukle Bernstein
Polish immigrant and landowner

Town REVEREND

DORIS

HARRY

RIFKA Bernstein
Moishe's wife

Seven BERNSTEIN CHILDREN
Four boys, two girls, and one infant

BERNIE
The shochet

YOUNG HARRY
A younger version of Harry

BOY 1

BOY 2

BOY 3

A POLICEMAN

ZEV
Russian farmer, a communist

Mr. HENLEY
Local politician

Mr. WILLARD
Local politician

HINDI
Moishe and Rifka's daughter

ANNIE Bernstein Manetta

CONSTABLE Niles

RIVEN
A Polish immigrant labourer

SAUL

FANYA

Mr. RICHARDSON
A baker

MR. JAMES
Editor of The Orono News

MRS. FANNING
Editorial assistant

JACK
A contractor building cottages

PATRICK
A young boy looking for his brother

HEAD NURSE
At quarantine

MRS. FRIEDMAN

JEFFREY
A young boy

EDDIE
A young boy

MINNIE
A young girl

SAM Manetta
Owner of Manetta's Resort and Doris's father

KID
A young boy, rescued from water

PEEWEE
Young Harry's friend

WOMAN
Sunbathing

MRS. EICHLER
A concerned mother

MRS. BORTS

MRS. SHLUMPSKY

MRS. ISKOWITZ

IDA
The hairdresser

YOUNG DORIS
A younger version of Doris

JACKIE Miller
A teenage boy

MAX
a Jewish Russian émigré

MARLIE
A teenage girl

ANNOUNCER
At Crystal's

LOUIE Weingarten,
aka Johnny Wayne
A comedian/singer

HERSHEL
A teenage boy

Nazi OFFICER

MR. SOLOMON

MR. SHERMAN

JD THOMAS
Ganaraska Watershed Visionary

FARMER

SAMMY CRYSTAL
Reporter

MAN 1

MAN 2

WOMAN 1

WOMAN 2

WOMAN 3

WEDDING OFFICIANT

MARTIN Applebaum
A teenage boy

RABBI

SHLOMO
A young boy

AARON
A young boy

MRS. BORAVSKY
A Polish émigré

MR. KAPNER
A Polish concentration camp survivor

MR. ROSENBLUM

MRS. ROSENBLUM

IRA Teitleman

DAVID Teitleman
A young boy

JOEL Teitleman
A young boy

MR. CALLAGHAN
Bank manager

Young MAN
Present day

Various other roles in background of scenes or as crowd members

Notes on Casting

This play can be produced with a minimum of ten actors playing multiple roles. Imagination is the key. It was originally produced with thirty-eight actors. More *is* better, but what can you do?

Casting for Ten Actors

This is one version of possible casting for the play:
Seven male, three female.
The play may be done with more than ten actors and males and females can be cast cross-gendered.

Act 1

Scene 1	Actor A (Moishe), Actor B (Irish Reverend)
Interlude 1	Actor C (Harry), Actor D (Doris), Actor E (Bernie), Actor F (Young Harry), Actor G (Boy 1), Actor E (Boy 2)
Scene 2	Actor A (Moishe), Actor G (Zev), Actor E (Henley), Actor B (Willard)
Scene 3	Actor A (Moishe), Actor H (Hindi), Actor E (Constable Niles), Actor B (Riven)
Scene 4	Actor A (Moishe), Actor I (Rifka)
Scene 5	Actor A (Moishe), Actor G (Butcher), Actor I (Shopper and Mrs. Golden), Actor B (Tailor), Actor F (Man), Actor E (Saul), Actor C (Grocer), Actor H (Fanya)
Scene 6	Actor I (Rifka), Actor H (Hindi), Actor B (Mr. Richardson)
Scene 7	Actor E (Mr. James), Actor H (Mrs. Fanning)
Scene 8	Actor A (Moishe), Actor I (Rifka), Actor H (Hindi), Actor G (Zev), Actor E (Jack), Actor F (Patrick)
Scene 9	Actor H (Nurse)
Scene 10	Actor A (Moishe), Actor I (Rifka)
Scene 10A	Actor A (Moishe), Actor I (Rifka), Actor B (Mr. Richardson)
Scene 11	Actor A (Moishe), Actor B (Sam Manetta), Actor G (Eddie), Actor H (Minnie / Mrs. Friedman), Actor I (Sunbather Mrs. Eichler), Actor F (Kid / Young Harry), Actor D (Old Doris), Actor C (Old Harry), Actor E (Saul), Actor J (Young Doris)

Scene 12	Actor I (Annie), Actor E (Mrs. Borts), Actor J (Mrs. Shlumpsky), Actor H (Mrs. Iskowitz), Actor G (Ida), Actor B (Sam), Actor D (Doris)
Scene 13	Train station – General noise
Scene 14	Actor J (Young Doris), Actor G (Jackie)
Scene 15	Actor I (Annie), Actor B (Sam), Actor J (Young Doris), Actor F (Young Harry)
Scene 16	Actor A (Moishe), Actor B (Sam), Actor G (Zev), Actor E (Max), Actor F (Young Harry)
Scene 17	Actor J (Young Doris), Actor F (Young Harry), Actor H (Marlie)
Scene 18	Actor C (Announcer), Actor A (Louie Weingarten), Actor F (Herschel), Everyone (Group Chorus)

Act 2

Scene 1	Train Station – Everyone stands, one at a time. Actor E (Nazi officer)
Scene 2	Actor I (Annie), Actor B (Sam), Actor J (Young Doris), Actor F (Young Harry), Actor C (Announcer), Actor G (Mr. Solomon), Actor E (Mr. Sherman)
Scene 3	Actor E (JD Thomas), Actor G (Farmer), Actor I (Woman 1), Actor H (Woman 2/Woman 3), Actor A (Sammy Crystal), Actor B (Man 1), Actor C (Man 2)
Scene 4	The Wedding. Actor G (Officiate), Actor B (Groom), Actor E (Bride), Everyone (Group Chorus)
Scene 5	Actor J (Young Doris), Actor H (Marlie), Actor E (Martin Applebaum)
Scene 6	Actor C (Rabbi), Actor A (Shofarist), Everyone (Group Chorus Adon Olam)
Scene 7	Actor J (Young Doris), Actor A (Shlomo), Actor F (Aaron), Actor G (Eddie), Actor H (Mrs. Friedman), Actor I (Mrs. Boravsky), Actor A (Eddie Kapner)
Scene 8	Actor E (Mr. Rosenblum), Actor H (Mrs. Rosenblum), Actor I (Annie), Actor B (Sam), Actor J (Young Doris), Actor C (Ira), Actor G (David), Actor A (Joel)
Scene 9	Actor E (Mr. Callaghan), Actor B (Sam)
Scene 10	Actor J (Young Doris)
Scene 11	Actor I (Annie), Actor B (Sam)
Scene 12	Actor C (Harry) Actor D (Doris) Actor F (Man) Voices 1–12

Setting

The action of the play takes place between 1905 and 2005 in and around Pontypool and Toronto, Ontario.

Playwright's Notes

I've probably said enough already, but I can't resist an opening, so here goes. I loved writing this play, Pontypool – a mini Catskills outside of Toronto, who knew? While working on this play I was amazed to discover how many people, Jews and non-Jews had a connection to Pontypool. I grew up in Montreal and my parents summered in the Laurentians, but their story is the same story. A small ethnic minority makes a little splash in an established community and the world changes. Immigrants struggling to make a dollar, get out of the city, enjoy a little time away, families connect, friendships endure, cultures intersect, new paths are carved and memories linger. Sounds like the history of Canada, no?

4th Line Theatre is a theatrical jewel. It is unique in the Canadian theatre ecology and the community involvement and support it receives is staggering. In addition to the effect the theatre has on so many lives, 4th Line produces stories that tell the history of the region in compelling and fascinating productions and I have been privileged to have so much of my work produced there. If you haven't been down Zion Line in Cavan township, what are you waiting for?

ACT ONE
Scene 1 (Prologue): 1916

In the distance there is a lone man (MOISHE) on a wagon being led by a horse. The wagon approaches, then stops. MOISHE looks around. A REVEREND appears.

MOISHE: (*With a Polish accent.*) Excuse me, mister. I think I'm lost. Is this the right road to Lindsay?

REVEREND: Lindsay? No sir, this road goes to Pontypool. Just over that hill.

MOISHE: Pontypool? (Where the hell is Pontypool?) I'm sorry. I don't got no map.

REVEREND: You sound a long way from home. (*Beat.*) Well, you can make it to Lindsay in the morning, it's not far. Pontypool has everything you need. You can get a nice pork chop and potato at the Coulter House and I can fix you a bed in the church, if you don't mind sleeping on the floor.

MOISHE: A pork supper and a church hotel. I must be in paradise.

REVEREND: The manse is down the main street. Knock on my door, if you'd like some help.

MOISHE: Thank you, mister. Thank you very much. I'll just rest my horse a minute.

The REVEREND leaves. MOISHE pulls out a carrot.

(*To the horse.*) This was going to be your supper, *tatala,* not mine. (*He takes a bite.*) Well, let's find a place to sleep. We'll get to Lindsay in the morning – God willing. Hyeah!

Interlude 1

DORIS and HARRY appear. DORIS begins to read from a storybook. (The two speak directly to the audience and occasionally interact with each other.)

DORIS: "Once upon a time there was a happy kingdom where the people lived in peace and everyone had enough to eat. The end."

She closes the book.

That's not a very Jewish story.

Jewish stories never go that way. Jewish stories are more like –

"Living under the evil Czar, the Jews were forbidden to pray on pain of death. So they met when there was no moon, in filthy basements and empty grottos to worship."

That's a Jewish story.

HARRY: Or there's this one. "The Rabbi of Limple was looking for a wife. His friend Eliazer suggested his sister Lada as a bride. True, Lada wasn't much to look at, Eliazer admitted, but she was honest, patient, and she cooked and cleaned like an angel. The rabbi, not wanting to hurt his friend's feelings, thought for a moment, took Ben Eliazer's hand and said, "The holy one promises that there will be plenty of angels when we get to heaven, so during my time on earth, if you don't mind, I'd prefer a pretty girl.

DORIS: Now, that's a Jewish story! I know, I heard plenty. Every summer for twenty years. In Pontypool.

HARRY: *Pontypool*. A no place in the middle of nowhere.

DORIS: Where I was born. I'll tell you how it got its name. There were two towns side by side, one called Ponty, one called Pool. They merged.

HARRY: Pretty exciting, huh?

DORIS: For most of the year it was a sleepy little town. There was never much of anything going on. But in the summer, boy, I tell you, I lived ten lifetimes for every one of those summers. I was just a kid, a *pisher*, underfoot all the time. Then I graduated to garbage man, then lifeguard and finally chief dishwasher. In Pontypool I learned just about everything I know.

HARRY: You went to university.

DORIS: Sure, but those summers….. All the people.. the... You remember… what was…. The, the, the comedian. He was very funny.

HARRY: Johnny Wayne.

DORIS: Johnny Wayne! From Wayne and Shuster. He used to perform in Pontypool.

HARRY: He was Jewish. He used to be Louie Weingarten. Then he hit the big time.

DORIS: *The Ed Sullivan Show.*

HARRY: That was a million years ago. When Napoleon wore short pants.

DORIS: The best times of my life. Come on, admit it. We were young, free. I'm not sentimental; well, I don't think I am, but what can I say? So much happened here, so many lives changed and now….it's gone.

HARRY: It was, in its heyday, a poor man's version of the Catskills in New York, or the Laurentians near Montreal with their Jewish resorts and beaches. Though Pontypool only had pine trees and a little pond – a pond, you couldn't even call it a pond – it was like a little bit of spit in a cup; the air was dry and the landscape was mediocre.

DORIS: It was beautiful. My cousin Harry forgets.

HARRY: Please. You could grow potatoes, tobacco, or maybe Christmas trees. You could watch cows standing around, or a grain elevator fire, but I wouldn't really call it beautiful.

DORIS: Not in the geographic sense, but it's the people who make a place worth living. Go find your little cabin in the Rockies with the glaciers and the sunsets.

HARRY: – I'd love to.

DORIS: – And see if living without good people, willing to do anything for you at the drop of a hat, isn't something you miss.

HARRY: All right, all right.

DORIS: And Pontypool was like that, even before the Jews went to holiday there. It was a village, a, a whatchamacallit.

HARRY: A *shtetl.*

DORIS: A *shtetl,* as our grandfather, our *zeida,* used to say.

MOISHE appears.

He grew up in a *shtetl* in Yvansk, Poland, so he knew.

MOISHE's family appears – his wife RIFKA and their seven children. RIFKA carries an infant. The others carry luggage for travel. A photograph is taken of the family. They go off.

Life was hard in Europe. He and Rifka, my bubba, knew what it was to raise a family and they knew how lucky they were to get out of Poland. And Pontypool was as good a place as any to begin again.

HARRY: There was nothing going on. It was tiny.

DORIS: It was tiny, but the town worked. It worked because the people worked together. That's why Pontypool prospered.

HARRY: Doris, it prospered, if you'll forgive me, because of the cottage industry. You forget that...

(*To audience.*) Now, when I say cottage industry, I don't mean *cottage industry* – as in the making of goods fashioned at home. No. I mean the building and rental of cottages, is what I mean. The cottages started out small. But then they went gangbusters.

DORIS: They were always building.

HARRY: First some ramshackle rooms built from old chicken coops and then a few sparse cottages, some with little *kuchelane,* little kitchens. Until finally, they were building resorts with swimming pools and entertainment, and big *kosher* dining rooms. It was really something.

DORIS: You think they know from *kosher?* They don't know.

HARRY: Sure they know.

DORIS. Harry! Tell them. (*Beat.*)

HARRY: You know what? Let Bernie, the *schochet,* do it.

BERNIE the shochet (ritual slaughterer) appears wearing an apron covered in blood, holding a cleaver.

BERNIE: *Kosher* is the ways the Jews eat. No meat and milk products together. No hindquarter of the animal. And no pork! No ham, no bacon, no pork chops. *Nisht*. And no shellfish…

HARRY: Boy, I love shellfish. Shrimp, crab, scampi.

DORIS: Lobster.

HARRY: You name it. So delicious!

DORIS: But you're not supposed to eat it.

HARRY: Ah! God can be so cruel.

BERNIE: Do you mind. (*Beat.*) *Kosher* is also the way the Jews kill their animals. It's the least painful way for the animal to die.

HARRY: *You slit its throat and let all the blood drip out.*

DORIS: Harry, there's children!

HARRY: They like gross stuff. I liked gross stuff when I was a kid. Boy. I saw a lot of gross stuff. When you serve as many duck dinners as we did on a Sunday afternoon, you see a lot of gross stuff.

BERNIE: You start killing them Saturday evening after *Shabbus* – (*With HARRY.*) *Slit their throats and let all the blood drip out.*

HARRY: *Gross!* Then they're plucked and gutted, seasoned and prepared for the salivating masses awaiting my Auntie Annie's famous Sunday feast.

DORIS: My mother prepared five hundred duck dinners every Sunday afternoon.

HARRY: That's a lot of ducks.

BERNIE: Excuse me. (*Beat.*) I got a date with a turkey.

BERNIE leaves.

DORIS: In its heyday, all over Pontypool. At Manetta's, at Crystal's Resort, Lofchick's strictly kosher, everywhere, there had to be twenty-five hundred Jews eating duck dinners before heading back to Toronto – to the Junction, to to to.....

HARRY: Spadina.

DORIS: Spadina. To Kensington Market.

HARRY: The multicultural world.

DORIS: What multicultural? It was all Jewish.

Beat.

HARRY: It was a joke.

DORIS: That was a joke? And I wanna say, for the record, that there was never any anti-Semitism in Pontypool. The Protestant people were all very nice. The communities worked side by side, helped each other. For a town with only a few permanent Jewish residents, they made us feel very welcome.

HARRY: I remember getting beaten up all the time.

DORIS: What are you talking about?

HARRY: Sure. They'd call you Jew-ball or Christ-killer, all those insults. I didn't even know what they meant.

DORIS: What are you talking.....?

Young HARRY runs on, winded. He finds a place to hide, breathing heavily.

Three young boys run on looking for him. Taunting.

BOY 1: Jew boy, hey Jew boy.

BOY 2: If we find you, you're dead.

BOY 3: Come on, Harry, we just wanna play baseball.

BOY 2: You mean matzoh ball.

BOY 3: Yeah, matzoh ball! (*Beat.*) What's a matzoh ball?

BOY 2: I don't know.

BOY 1: Hey Jew-ball, come out, come out, wherever you are.

The boys see HARRY. HARRY runs off, the boys follow him.

Get him, don't let him get away.

DORIS: That never happened.

HARRY: You remember what you want to remember, Doris.

DORIS: I don't even remember what I had for breakfast.

HARRY: I'd get two or three of them on me, holding me down, spitting in my face. I came home with plenty of shiners. Believe me. I mean nobody burned crosses or anything, they were just being kids. But at the July 12th Orange Parade, I'll tell you, we were pretty glad we weren't Catholic.

DORIS: They don't want to hear that.

HARRY: All right. Listen. I'll tell you something. When the whole cottage thing started, it was prohibition, so no one could take a drink. Manvers was a dry township.

A POLICEMAN walks the beat. MOISHE walks by with a sack that says "Barley." He nods at the officer, the officer nods back.

My *zeida*...

DORIS: Well they say he had a whiskey still on his property, but they never found it.

HARRY: ...he had one.

DORIS: There were rumours, that he buried it, that he blew it up, that he put it in a box and mailed it to the prime minister, but no one knows if he really had one or not.

HARRY: He had one…

DORIS: My cousin Harry will tell you different, of course, just to be difficult.

HARRY: Doris.

DORIS: I don't know.

HARRY: I saw it.

DORIS: I never saw *Zeida* take a drink.

MOISHE removes a tarp from a table. Under it is a whiskey still. MOISHE opens the spigot and takes a drink.

HARRY: *Zeida* was no saint, Doris. They say when he buried his whiskey still, he gave it a proper funeral with a prayer shawl and a prayer book. Maybe he made a map.

DORIS: Yeah.

HARRY: What a character.

DORIS: Moishe Yukle Bernstein. He came to Toronto 1905. Sold clothes in a wagon, ran a pant factory in the Junction. On Maria Street.

HARRY: Mah-rye-ah Street.

DORIS: Maria, Mah-rye-ah. Who cares.

HARRY: By the synagogue there, Knesset Israel, oldest in Ontario.

DORIS: And finally, he became a peddler travelling between Peterborough and Lindsay. He saw land was cheap in Pontypool, so he bought the place that belonged to the uh, the…..uh….

HARRY: Jennings.

DORIS: John and Amelia Jennings, the folks who founded Pontypool.

HARRY: Moishe Yukle Bernstein. They called him Moishe, they called him Yukle, they called him Bernie. But they never called him "late for dinner." (*Beat.*) That was a joke, too.

DORIS: He sold clothes in a wagon, he ran a pant factory in... Did I mention that? (*Beat.*) Anyway. He was busy with every little thing.

HARRY: He was a real operator. Once he settled in Pontypool, he was *schmoozing* with the local politicians like nobody's business. He knew everybody.

Scene 2: Zev's Farm, 1917

MOISHE speaks in a Polish accent as does ZEV. HENLEY is the local politician running for election. ZEV is cutting wood.

MOISHE: Zev, put down the axe. (*Beat.*) Zev, put down a minute, come here.

ZEV: Yukle. How's by you?

MOISHE: Can't complain. Well, I could, but who would hear it?

ZEV: God.

MOISHE: Sure, but he wouldn't do nothing about it. Zev, I want you should meet Mr. *Ch*enley, he is running for council in the township and I told him he can have your vote.

HENLEY: It's *Henley*, actually.

MOISHE: I told him, of course, we feel welcome in the township, we are happy to support our politicians. Mr. *Ch*enley wants your support for the election.

ZEV: Nice to meet you, Mr. *Ch*enley.

HENLEY: It's *Henley*.

ZEV: This is what I say, *Ch*enley.

HENLEY: With an "H."

ZEV: Sure, *Chenley* with an *H*. So what would you like?

HENLEY: Like? Well, I'd like your vote on election day, Mr. Zev. May 14th.

ZEV: What for?

HENLEY: Well, uh, because voting is how we elect representatives in our democratic system.

ZEV: Yes, I know – democracy, the golden age of Greece. But why I should vote for you? What good will it do me?

MOISHE: Be pleasant, Zev.

HENLEY: That's all right, Bernie. It's a tumultuous time in the world, Mr. Zev. There's war in Europe, the rise of Bolshevism in Russia. We in Manvers Township want to ensure our community is doing all it can for our soldiers and to support Prime Minister Borden's conscription initiative.

ZEV: Conscription?

HENLEY: Drafting soldiers into the army.

ZEV: Ah.

MOISHE: Like the Czar's army, right, Mr. *Ch*enley?

HENLEY: Er…ah, I guess so.

MOISHE: They take from the family the best and youngest men and put them to fight in the war, no?

HENLEY: Yes.

ZEV: What for?

HENLEY: Why, to save the world from the terrible threats that face it, Mr. Zev. Famine, poverty, war.

ZEV: They go to war to stop war.

HENLEY: Yes, exactly. And with your vote, Mr. Zev, we will win this war and eliminate the dangers that face our country. Our township.

MOISHE: (*Looking at his watch.*) Okay, Mr. *Ch*enley, Zev votes for you, I votes for you. I talk to more Slavs in Manvers. Vote *Ch*enley, stop Bolshevism!

HENLEY: Yes, Moishe. Thank you. It's *Henley*. Nice to meet you, Mr. Zev. We should go, Moishe, there's more farmers to canvass.

MOISHE: You go, Mr. *Ch*enley. I will tell Poles, Russians "Vote *Ch*enley" but now I must milk my cow.

HENLEY: I thought we would visit more…

MOISHE: I will make a meeting. We will help you, Mr. *Ch*enley. Don't worry. (*Beat.*)

HENLEY: All right. Thank you. (*He starts to go.*)

MOISHE: *Ch*enley? You have the uh…..?

HENLEY: Huh? Oh yes. Here you go. (*He gives him some money. Then, quietly.*) Spread the word, Moishe. There's plenty more where that came from.

MOISHE: It's a pleasure doing business with you, Mr. *Ch*enley.

HENLEY: Goodbye.

HENLEY leaves.

ZEV: What's wrong with Bolshevism? The workers are together. Socialist. If I could go back I would go. I don't like him.

MOISHE: Don't worry, he won't win. Vote how you like. (*Beat.*)

ZEV: Moishe. You maybe want to share a little, the money?

MOISHE: What for?

ZEV: I have things to pay for, too.

MOISHE: Zev, you're a communist, you stay true to your principles. I don't want you should compromise yourself.

ZEV: Listen, I came to this country to…..

Enter Mr. Edmond WILLARD.

WILLARD: Ah, Mr. Moishe, I've been looking for you. We've a lot of people to meet if we're going to win this election. Hello, Edmond Willard, running for council, and may I say, unlike a lot of the candidates, I am pro-immigration. It's immigrants that built this country and I hope I can count on your support.

MOISHE: Zev, this is Mr. Willard, he's running for council in the township and I told him he can have your vote.

Interlude 2

DORIS: In those days you had to eke out a living somehow and Moishe was no farmer. He'd have better luck getting milk from chickens and eggs from cows, if you know what I mean. But with a little ingenuity they managed.

HARRY: A little graft went a long way.

DORIS: Harry!

HARRY: At that time it was different, see, because the government didn't want Jews to come to Canada. But they needed farmers. So Moishe helped friends and family leave Poland by applying for visas for them to come over here and work as farm labourers.

A GROUP OF IMMIGRANTS appear. They pass through customs at Pier 21.

ANNOUNCEMENT OVER LOUDSPEAKER:

Welcome to Halifax. Please have your papers ready for inspection.

Ukrainians, Poles, and Litvaks to the left, Ruthenians, Bohemians, and Russians to the right.

Do not cross the yellow line. Welcome to Halifax.

HARRY: These people didn't know from farm work. They were needlers. Tailors and seamstresses and cutters of *shmatas.* Rags.

The workers open up their suitcases and begin to sew and measure cloth. A sewing machine appears. We hear the stitching.

It was the rag trade. What's a poor Jew with nothing going to do, but make a living out of rags.

DORIS: And it worked. They came over as farm workers and they made their way to Toronto. To work in the sewing trade, in sweatshops and factories.

HARRY: It was big.

DORIS: There was a whole community. Around College and Spadina there. What's that place? Near the Harbord Bakery.

HARRY: That's not where the Harbord Bakery is.

DORIS: Where's the Harbord Bakery?

HARRY: On Harbord.

DORIS: It was in..... Oh what do they call it?

HARRY: Kensington Market.

DORIS: Kensington Market. How could I forget.

HARRY: Like from *King of Kensington.*

DORIS: They don't remember that.

HARRY: It was a TV show. With Al Waxman – *allava shalom.* He was Jewish. (*Beat.*) So anyway, the Jews filled Kensington Market with their joys and woes and they sewed. Businesses built up with screaming chickens and geese.

DORIS: Cheese shops, bakeries, a synagogue.

HARRY: And the garment industry blossomed. Spilled out of Kensington Market onto the Spadina Street and filled its tenements and warehouses –

DORIS: – with hat shops and furriers –

HARRY: – and shoes and bags and luggage shops.

DORIS: It was wonderful. You knew everybody. Everybody knew you. *Oy.* (*Beat.*) But anyway, back in Pontypool, Moishe knew a lot of people.

HARRY: Politicians. The chief of police, the president of the Independent Order of Odd Fellows.

DORIS: And they would warn him when the RCMP was coming to inspect his farm for immigration infractions. And Moishe would immediately get word to Toronto and that night, a bunch of tailors dressed as farmers would be on the train back to Pontypool.

Scene 3: Bernstein Farm, outside.

Workers are in the field. HINDI enters with her younger sister, ANNIE. There is a whiskey still on a table.

HINDI: Papa, someone's here to see you. From the RCMP.

MOISHE: Hindi.

HINDI: Yes, Papa.

MOISHE: You came in after nine last night.

HINDI: Hannah and I were darning socks for the soldiers.

MOISHE: It's too late for a girl to be out.

HINDI: Papa, the sun doesn't even set until –

MOISHE: You're arguing?

HINDI: No, Papa.

MOISHE: It won't happen again.

HINDI: No, Papa. (*Beat.*) Except, tonight is Hannah's birthday and –

MOISHE: And what?

HINDI: If I could just stay until they shoot off the fireworks.

MOISHE: Fireworks? What do you need with fireworks? Your brothers aren't out all night. Neither is Eva. Annie, what about you? Are you out till all hours?

ANNIE: No, Papa.

HINDI: Please, Papa. Please? She's my best friend, pleeeease.

MOISHE: I should give you a spanking.

HINDI: Papa.

MOISHE: You, you're like a worm that crawls in my heart.

HINDI: Thank you, Papa.

MOISHE: Just this once.

HINDI: Of course, Papa.

MOISHE: Give me a kiss. You too, monkey.

The girls kiss him and leave. MOISHE covers the whiskey still with a tarp and pretends to do some work. CONSTABLE Niles enters.

CONSTABLE: Mr. Bernstein.

MOISHE: Constable Niles. So how's tricks?

CONSTABLE: A lot of field hands you've got there, Mr. Bernstein.

MOISHE: Good workers, they like to work with their hands.

CONSTABLE: What are you going to plant this year?

MOISHE: Maybe potatoes.

CONSTABLE: Potatoes, eh.

MOISHE: Maybe hay for the animals.

CONSTABLE: There's a big difference between hay and potatoes.

MOISHE: Whatever makes the best price.

CONSTABLE: I see. All those people work for you?

MOISHE: Of course.

CONSTABLE: Where do they sleep?

MOISHE: In the summer kitchen, the barn. Some sleep outside. The weather is nice.

CONSTABLE: What happens when it rains?

Dov Mickelson as Moishe Yukle Bernstein, on the road to Pontypool.

Moishe Yukle Bernstein (Dov Mickelson) hugs his daughters.

MOISHE: They get wet.

CONSTABLE: Un-huh. Any of them Canadian citizens?

MOISHE: Everyone is Canadian.

CONSTABLE: They have papers?

MOISHE: Sure, how else they come with no papers?

CONSTABLE: You! Hey you. Come here.

RIVEN enters.

RIVEN: (*Polish accent.*) Yes?

CONSTABLE: You work here?

RIVEN: Yes, sir.

CONSTABLE: How long?

RIVEN: 1916.

CONSTABLE: Let me see your papers. Un huh. From Kiv, Ukraine, eh?

RIVEN: Kiev.

CONSTABLE: You live here? In Pontypool.

RIVEN: Yes, sir. Work for Mr. Bernstein.

CONSTABLE: You're a farm worker?

RIVEN: Yes, sir.

CONSTABLE: It says here you're a hat maker. You see, under "Trade." "Hat Maker."

RIVEN: If I find straw I make hats. Now I am a farm worker.

CONSTABLE: You married?

RIVEN: That's my wife Manya and my boys.

CONSTABLE: Which ones?

RIVEN: All of them. Seven boys.

CONSTABLE: Seven?

MOISHE: His wife's a hard worker, too.

CONSTABLE: All right. Bernstein, for a guy with so many workers, I haven't seen a harvest on this land yet.

MOISHE: Drought.

CONSTABLE: Drought, eh?

MOISHE: And crows.

CONSTABLE: Drought and crows. You know, Bernstein....

MOISHE: Oh, Constable. (*Quietly.*) You know, next to my property, in the field on the *other* side of the fence, I think I saw, I'm not sure, but maybe there was a jug of whiskey someone left. I don't know. Me, I don't drink, but I think someone left it there and don't want it no more. I don't know. Maybe check and see, none of my business.

CONSTABLE: Thanks, Bernstein, I'll check it out.

MOISHE: Maybe they left a few cigars too, I don't know, I don't pay attention.

CONSTABLE: I'll do an inspection. Make sure everything is.... *kosher*.

CONSTABLE Niles leaves. MOISHE pulls a flask out of his pocket and takes a nip.

MOISHE: I'm sure it is.

Scene 4: Bernstein Kitchen

MOISHE is making notes in a book.

RIFKA: You look tired.

MOISHE: I'm fine.

RIFKA: You hardly ate nothing. I made you *borscht.*

MOISHE: I'll eat later.

RIFKA: What's the matter?

MOISHE: Nothing. (*Beat.*) Trying to make a living, that's the matter.

RIFKA: We're okay. In Poland you could make a living? Here you have a house and land, there you live in a shack with a straw roof, with the animals coming in. Piss-poor.

MOISHE: I know.

RIFKA: This is the land of money, Yukle. You'll make enough.

MOISHE: How? I'm gonna print it myself? That's the only way.

RIFKA: What are you complaining? You have Cossacks coming and destroying everything?

MOISHE: Again with the Cossacks.

RIFKA: Stealing and raping and burning children.

MOISHE: Rifka, all right.

RIFKA: For my cousin Nettie, *allavashalom,* it's all right? For her dead babies it's all right? Please. What if it was our Annie? Here we have a chance. They don't kill Jews for nothing. There, to go in the street is to take your life in your hands. You're a smart man, Yukle, you'll make a dollar, don't worry.

MOISHE: How about a million dollars?

RIFKA: How about ten dollars. Since when are you a dreamer?

Beat.

MOISHE: The children are home?

RIFKA: Annie and Eva are asleep, the boys are upstairs.

MOISHE: And Hindi? Rifka?

RIFKA: She's at the Himmelfarbs'.

MOISHE: So late?

RIFKA: I'll get you some *borscht.*

MOISHE: She's like a wild horse, that one. I should put a rope around her. (*Beat.*) Rifka.

RIFKA: What?

MOISHE: Mottle and Sarah are coming up from Toronto, Friday.

RIFKA: What for?

MOISHE: Delicious.

RIFKA: What for?

MOISHE: I told them, come for a few days.

RIFKA: With the children?

MOISHE: Sure with the children, what then?

RIFKA: Moishe, where are we going to put them? Why didn't you tell me? You have seven children, you're going to raise theirs too? And what are they going to eat? I have to buy, I have nothing.

MOISHE: So we'll get! They can sleep in the summer kitchen! on the floor! Sarah has the asthma, the air is good for her.

RIFKA: My husband and his ideas. Next time you invite people to stay and eat our food, ask for a few dollars, hunh? You want to be a rich man? Stop paying for everyone else!

Interlude 3

DORIS: And that was it. Like at the races when they open the gate, they were off.

Moishe invited friends up to Pontypool and on Rifka's insistence, they paid. Not much, five dollars for five people to eat and sleep for a few days, but every little bit helped.

Kensington Market is recreated. It is lively, filled with animals, people, and music.

HARRY: And *Zeida* Moishe started going back and forth to Toronto all the time to invite more people. It was a little business. The beds weren't comfortable, you had no privacy, but the food was good, and then like now, it was good to get out of the city. Toronto gets so hot.

Scene 5: Kensington Market, 1918

Voices, music, noise.

BUTCHER: I got chickens, live chickens! Killed fresh with *pipikles* and gizzards.

I got briskets, flanken, rib steaks, veal chops, fresh and delicious.

SHOPPER: You got turnips?

GROCER: I've got celery and parsnips. That's it.

SHOPPER: I'm making a soup, I need turnips.

TAILOR: You want a suit I can make you a suit but not for peanuts. You want a suit made from peanuts, go see Caplansky, I only make the best. Don't waste my time.

MOISHE: Saul, Saul, is that you? Saul. You look terrible.

SAUL: Yukle. You're back in Toronto?

MOISHE: Just on business.

SAUL: We could use an organizer downtown, Yukle.

MOISHE: Saul.

SAUL: The men looked up to you at the pant factory.

MOISHE: I'm not interested in unions. You know what I'm organizing now?

SAUL: What?

MOISHE: Your vacation. Solly, you need to get out of town. Get some sun. You look like tapioca.

SAUL: I can't afford to go away.

MOISHE: It'll cost you *bupkas*. You bring Essie and the kids. You stay three days, you won't recognize yourself.

SAUL: You're a real capitalist now.

MOISHE: I'm a Yukle-ist. I do what's good for Yukle.

MOTHER: Izzy, don't touch that.

IZZY: But Mama.

MOTHER: Don't "Mama" me, I said don't touch!

SAUL: Yukle, Horatio Hocken was a strike organizer and he became Mayor of Toronto. You like politics, you know people. You work for the party, all your dreams could come true. Communism is the future.

MOISHE: I'm looking after today, the future I'll worry about tomorrow.

SAUL: Yukle.

MOISHE: How's the rheumatism, Solly?

SAUL: It's killing me. I don't sleep at night.

MOISHE: Three days in Pontypool, your leg will be brand new, I guarantee.

SAUL: I want to laugh, I'll read the newspaper.

MOISHE: The air is magic, Solly, and the pond has healing powers.

SAUL: Healing.

MOISHE: It's a *mechia*. What have you got to lose, but the pain in your *tuchas*. Come see for yourself. Here's the address.

GROCER: You gonna pay for that apple?

SHOPPER: I'm testing it. I want to make a strudel.

GROCER: First you buy, then you test. *Gay avek*, you *gonuf*!

MOISHE: (*Seeing some people.*) Fanya, Manny, you look terrible. What are you still doing in the city?

FANYA: Who can afford to go away?

MOISHE: Who can afford not to. Look at this advertisement. You pay five dollars, you feel like a million dollars. All your meals included, transportation. I drive you in my *trockele.* Beautiful countryside. Take a look. Excuse me.

TAILOR: Mrs. Golden, I told you Thursday.

MRS. GOLDEN: So, today is Thursday.

TAILOR: I meant the Thursday after this Thursday.

MOISHE: Tzvi? Tzvi Lepelski? You look like you died. How's the apartment? Sticky, I'll bet? Ah, the city stinks. You know what you need.....take a look at this.

Interlude 4

DORIS: Moishe sold Pontypool like the Garden of Eden. Toronto was a torture chamber. The beaches at Sunnyside were packed at night, they were sleeping in rows by the hundreds.

HARRY: And remember, most places were closed to Jews. Some beaches said "No dogs or Jews allowed."

DORIS: But here in Pontypool, they had open space, fresh air, and when the heat was too much there was the lake.

HARRY: It was a pond. Full of leeches, flies, and snakes.

DORIS: So it wasn't the French Riviera, it was the Jewish Riviera. For poor people who couldn't afford anything else, Pontypool was *the* vacation spot. And the townsfolk didn't mind. There was a little more business and that was good for the economy.

Scene 6: Mr. Richardson's Bakery

RIFKA: Mr. Richardson, how's by you?

RICHARDSON: Fine, thanks, Mrs. Bernstein. Hello, Miss Bernstein.

HINDI: Mr. Richardson.

RICHARDSON: What can I get for you, Mrs. Bernstein?

RIFKA: Six loaves bread, please.

RICHARDSON: Six?

HINDI: We have guests coming again.

RICHARDSON: I only have five.

RIFKA: Five? – *Sis nisht genig.* (*It's not enough.*) Okay, give me five.

RICHARDSON: I can only give you three, I have to keep two for Mrs. White.

RIFKA: Three? *Vos ken ich teen?* (*What can I do?*)

HINDI: It's not enough, Mama. *Vilst epes onderish?* (*You want something else?*)

RIFKA: You got something else?

RICHARDSON: What do you want?

RIFKA: You don't got no bagels, hunh?

RICHARDSON: What?

HINDI: Bagels.

RICHARDSON: What's that?

HINDI: Bagel? *Vus is a bagel?* (*What's a bagel?*) It's round, with a hole in the middle.

Beat.

RICHARDSON: You mean *olykoeks.* (*Ol-ee-cooks.*) Fried dough. "Dough-nuts" the kids call 'em.

RIFKA: Not fried, baked.

RICHARDSON: Baked?

RIFKA: You mix dough with egg, oil, salt, roll in circle, boil in honey water, dip in poppy seeds and you bake.

RICHARDSON: Never heard of that, Mrs. Bernstein. I don't imagine you'll ever find those around here. How about something sweet?

RIFKA: Sweet? *Vos is* sweet?

HINDI: *Zees.*

RIFKA: *Zees.* You got *rogalach?*

RICHARDSON: No.

RIFKA: *Tagalach?*

RICHARDSON: No.

RIFKA: Strudel? Honey cake? *Muhn* cookies?

RICHARDSON: Uh, I don't think so.

HINDI: What have you got, Mr. Richardson?

RICHARDSON: I've got number cakes, meringues, and one last banana bread –

RIFKA: Banana bread?

RICHARDSON: Yup.

Beat.

RIFKA: What's a banana?

Scene 7: *The Orono News* Office

MR. JAMES, who is Scottish, and MRS. FANNING are at the office of The Orono News.

MR. JAMES: Mrs. Fanning, have you got the finals?

MRS. FANNING: Your spelling is abysmal, Mr. James. You spelt Methodist with an "R."

MR. JAMES: Really? "*Merthodist.*" (*Beat.*) It might catch on. The Merthodists of Orono.

MRS. FANNING: You might start your own religion.

MR. JAMES: There's enough religion without any new ones. (*Beat.*) You used to know who people were. Now…

MRS. FANNING: What?

MR. JAMES: All these immigrants. With their languages and practices.

MRS. FANNING: Canada is a land of immigrants, Mr. James.

MR. JAMES: Of course, we're all immigrants, Mrs. Fanning. But at least we were English and Scottish. Now there's Russians, Dutch, Polish.

MRS. FANNING: They have the same right to be here as us.

MR. JAMES: No doubt, Mrs. Fanning. But *The Orono News* isn't going to read itself. All right, read me what you've got.

MRS. FANNING: Item. "The Kennedy grain elevator will be fitted up by the Good Grain Company of Toronto, to replace the elevator destroyed by fire last week." Item. "Work started Monday, building the cement foundation of the new *Methodist* Church."

MR. JAMES: Methodist is good, stick with that.

MRS. FANNING: "The church will be complete by mid-August."

MRS. FANNING: Item. "On Wednesday Mr. Nelson McMullen was married to Miss Flo Wells. The young couple will make their home at Ballyduff."

MR. JAMES: I was quite fond of Flo Wells. Sweet young thing. Now she's married.

MRS. FANNING: You're more than twenty years her senior, Mr. James.

Beat.

MR. JAMES: Well, I never said she was fond of me. Read on.

MRS. FANNING: Item. "Mrs. Graham has been quite ill and her daughter, Mrs. Masters, has been waiting on her. She is now much improved." You know, she was suffering from a catarrh and Mrs. Himmelfarb cured her.

MR. JAMES: Mrs. Himmelfarb? How?

MRS. FANNING: Chicken soup.

MR. JAMES: Chicken soup?

MRS. FANNING: The Jewish people swear by it. They don't have doctors, they just take chicken soup when they're sick.

MR. JAMES: Peculiar.

MRS. FANNING: I understand Mrs. Himmelfarb is an excellent cook besides. All sorts of Polish delicacies.

MR. JAMES: I couldn't eat that. Stuffed cabbage and smelly pots of entrails. Uch. Give me a nice haggis and some blood pudding and I'm a happy man.

MRS. FANNING: Item. "Mr. Moishe Yukle Bernstein of Pontypool has built a few small cottages on his property to engage needle workers from Toronto in a pleasant relaxation spot. Said Yukle, 'It's a sure way to make a million dollars.' We believe he purchased the wood for the cottages from Ridges Hardware in Pontypool."

MR. JAMES: (*Sotto voce.*) He actually got it from Foster's Hardware here in Orono.

MRS. FANNING: Really?

MR. JAMES: I was at Foster's the day Ridges came by. Ridges had no planks left. Sold them to the grain elevator people. Ridges says the Jew wants to build some cottages and doesn't even know the cost of a plank of wood. So Foster and Ridges make a deal. Ridges sells Foster's planks to the Jew at twice the price and he and Foster split the profits.

Beat.

MRS. FANNING: Then Mr. Bernstein got the planks at Fosters, we should correct the item.

MR. JAMES: Leave it as is.

MRS. FANNING: But Mr. James. Our readers expect the truth.

MR. JAMES: Ridges got the wood from Foster and then sold it to the Jew. So as far the Jew knows, he bought the wood from Ridges, therefore it's not a lie. Besides, I owe Ridges some advertising. He gave me a deal on nails last week. Two cents a pound. (*Beat.*) Don't look at me like that. We have to look out for own kind, Mrs. Fanning. The bible tells us so. *The Orono News*. Real News for Real Canadians.

Scene 8: In the Field

MOISHE is in the field with RIFKA, ZEV, and some hired hands.

MOISHE: One two three!

They raise a cottage in the field.

Son of a gun. Look at that.

RIFKA: It's beautiful. It'll get the morning light. *Doos vet zien a fargeneegen.*

MOISHE: Zev, get the shingles. You can start on the roof.

JACK: Hey Bernstein, I don't have your stove pipes.

MOISHE: What? I'm promising a *kuchelane.*

JACK: And I don't have your ceiling vents. They screwed up.

MOISHE: Who?

JACK: Toronto Building Supply. They're asleep at the switch. I tried all week to get supplies, but they didn't answer. They could have had a nice chunk of business but now I'm ordering from Kingston. It's more expensive, but they deliver on time.

ZEV: Moishe, my friend Joe in Lindsay has a hardware store. I can get you a deal.

JACK: I got a contact in Kingston, he'll help me out. Let me see if I need anything else.

ZEV: He'll deliver on the weekend, Moishe. He'll save you ten percent and free delivery.

MOISHE: I got people coming tomorrow.

ZEV: You'll save money. He's my friend. It's good to keep things in the community.

JACK: Spoken like a real communist. Don't worry, Bernie, we'll fix it up for ya.

ZEV: Moishe, everyone benefits if you…

MOISHE: Let Frank take care of it, Zev, please.

Beat.

ZEV: (*Sotto voce.*) Rifka, talk to him.

HINDI enters wearing a blanket, not looking well.

RIFKA: Hindi, you should be in bed.

HINDI: I'm fine, Mama. I want to see Papa's enterprise.

RIFKA: You'll catch a chill.

HINDI: I'm feeling better, really.

MOISHE: If we rent these cottages for six weeks, Hindi, I can buy you your own sewing machine.

HINDI: I don't want a sewing machine, Papa. I want a phonograph.

MOISHE: A phonograph?

HINDI: To play cylinders. Everyone has them now.

MOISHE: That's going to get you a husband?

HINDI: Papa, you're so old-fashioned.

ZEV: Moishe, I just have to make a call to Lindsay and….

PATRICK enters.

PATRICK: Good day, Mr. Bernstein. My mother wants me to bring Joe home.

RIFKA: Is everything alright?

PATRICK: She got a telegram, my brother Percy's gone missing.

Beat.

MOISHE: Of course, Patrick, he's in the barn.

HINDI: But the war is over.

JACK: Doesn't mean everyone's home yet. What's his outfit, son?

PATRICK: 3rd Peel Regiment, but he joined the RFC over there. He's a pilot.

JACK: Good for him. Maybe he shot down that Red Baron.

PATRICK: I don't know, sir.

JACK: Good luck to you, son. Hope he comes home soon. I'll go make that order, Bernie.

JACK exits.

RIFKA: Go get your brother, Pat. And tell Mrs. Chambers we wish her good news.

PATRICK: Thanks, ma'am.

PATRICK exits.

MOISHE: To hell with the Kaiser! (*He spits.*)

ZEV: Moishie, ten percent I can save you, that Frank will skin you like a cat.

MOISHE: Not in front of the girl, Zev, please. See if you can find some nails, I want to secure the front steps.

HINDI: Poor Percy. I hope they find him. I remember him in school he .... Ooh.

HINDI swoons.

RIFKA: Hindi? Hindilah, what is it?

HINDI: Mama. I don't...

RIFKA: What?

HINDI: I don't feel so well.

RIFKA: Moishe.

MOISHE: I've got her.

RIFKA: What's the matter?

HINDI: I'm dizzy.

RIFKA: She's burning up.

ZEV: Should I get the doctor?

HINDI: I'm freezing.

MOISHE: You went out last night with no sweater?

RIFKA: She went to Lucy's.

HINDI: Edgar's back from Belgium. He told us war stories.

RIFKA: Were you around anyone sick?

HINDI: No, Mama, no one was sick.

Scene 9: Quarantine

NURSES enter wearing masks.

HEAD NURSE: (*To audience.*) The quarantined will be isolated down at the park to reduce the spread. Thank you, Marge, for organizing the latrines. Schools, churches, theatres, and public places are all closed. We should also urge factory owners to send workers home who might be even mildly sick, so they don't infect anyone. Meg, we need to notify them of the influenza. The rest of you, we've cots to assemble and sheets to disinfect. Let's go, go, go.

Scene 10A

MOISHE, RIFKA, and their six children enter, devastated.

RIFKA stops. MOISHE goes to her, tries to get her to move.

MOISHE: Rifka, come.

RIFKA: Hindi. My Hindi.

MOISHE: Rifka....the others need a mother too.

Beat. ANNIE, the youngest child, crosses to RIFKA.

RIFKA: We never should have come here.

RIFKA falls to her knees and begins to weep.

We never should have come.

ANNIE: Mama.

RIFKA looks at ANNIE, touches her face.

MOISHE: Let's go.

ANNIE takes RIFKA's hand and they move off.

Interlude 5

DORIS: It's the hardest thing, to bury a child.

HARRY: Amen.

DORIS: You sit *shiva* for seven days. But the mourning never ends. But when there's other children to look after and grandchildren, what do you do?

Scene 10B

MOISHE drinking whiskey, beside his whiskey still. He sings a melancholy little Yiddish lullaby.

In dem Beis-Hamikdosh
In a vinkl cheyder
Zitst di almone, bas-tsion, aleyn
Ihr ben yochidle yideln vigt zi keseider
Un zingt im tzum shlofn a ledeleh sheyn.
Ai-lu-lu

Unter Yidele's vigele
Shteyt a klor-vays tsigele
Dos tsigele iz geforn handlen
Dos vet zayn dayn baruf
Rozhinkes mit mandlen
Slof-zhe, Yidele, shlof.

(In the Temple,
in a corner of a room,
Sits the widowed daughter of Zion, alone.
She rocks her only son, Yidele, to sleep
With a sweet lullaby.
Ai-lu-lu

Under Yidele's cradle
Stands a small white goat.
The goat travelled to sell his wares
This will be Yidele's calling, too.
Trading in raisins and almonds.
Sleep, Yidele, sleep.)

RIFKA enters.

RIFKA: You're drinking again? What's the matter with you? We got people coming tonight.

MOISHE: I know.

RIFKA: You'll be drunk when they get here.

MOISHE: What does it matter?

RIFKA: What are you talking. Yukle, what's wrong? You're like a different person. I wish you'd get rid of this whiskey. You drink and it's like I don't know you anymore.

MOISHE: I don't even know myself.

RIFKA: What is it? Tell me.

Beat.

MOISHE: Such a beauty. Like my mother *alla-va-shalom…*

RIFKA: Not again. Enough, Yukle! Hindi's gone. We can't live for the dead. That's why we left Europe. We're alive, we have to make do. *You* told me that. We have work to do. Grandchildren to enjoy. That's what keeps us going. Now put away the drink, I made you lunch.

MOISHE: I'm not hungry.

RIFKA: Don't tell me. I have brisket and kasha.

Beat.

MOISHE: You got *vereneky?*

RIFKA: You think you're a Romanov? *Vereneky* every day.

MOISHE: I like *vereneky.*

RIFKA: I have a couple, I'll put in the oven. Come. Help me with the washing 'til it's ready.

Beat.

MOISHE: Rifka.

RIFKA: Yeah.

MOISHE: Sometimes I remember why I married you.

Mr. RICHARDSON appears.

RICHARDSON: Mrs. Bernstein, Mr. Bernstein, sorry to bother you.

RIFKA: Mr. Richardson, how's by you?

RICHARDSON: I've got something I want to show you.

Mr. RICHARDSON pulls out a large doughy bagel.

MOISHE: What is it?

RICHARDSON: It's a bah-gel. I remembered you told me about them, Mrs. Bernstein, and I made my own. Try it.

MOISHE and RIFKA try it.

What do you think?

MOISHE: My horse would like it.

RIFKA: Yukle! It's not bad, Mr. Richardson, but it needs something.

RICHARDSON: What?

RIFKA: Something Jewish.

MOISHE: Richardson, you want a drop of whiskey?

RIFKA: Yukle, we're going inside. Come, Mr. Richardson, I'll show you the recipe again. And you can have a *vereneky.*

RICHARDSON: What's a *vereneky?*

MOISHE: What's a *vereneky?* What's a *vereneky!* Oh boy, are you in for a treat.

Interlude 6

HARRY: *Zeida* Moishe. Like a businessman, got on with the business of living.

DORIS: There were the cottages to run, he had a family to look after: four boys, Eva...

HARRY: My mother.

DORIS: And little Annie, my mother.

HARRY: What else can you do? That's what life's about, the living. Otherwise, it's just canasta and tea socials. It moves from one generation to the next. It's called progress.

Scene 11: 1937

Music. The Pond/Manetta's Resort. (HARRY and DORIS watch and begin commenting during the following scenes.)

A BUNCH of CHILDREN run on in bathing suits. Singing and playing. OTHER VACATIONERS enter, milling about. We see people at the pond. A woman bent over, MRS. FRIEDMAN, enters.

EDDIE: "Mrs. Friedman bent her back, lives inside a fishing shack. Mrs. Friedman bent her spine, twisted like a spool of twine." You gonna take a dip in the pond? Hunh, Mrs. Friedman? Huh?

MRS. FRIEDMAN: Ah, shaddap!

MINNIE: The leeches aren't bad. Come on, Mrs. Friedman, I'll race you.

JEFFREY: Leave her alone. She's a nice old lady.

MRS. FRIEDMAN: If I could straighten out, I'd out-swim all of you.

EDDIE: Sure, you would. Sure, you would.

MRS. FRIEDMAN: I would! Odessa city champion. Three years in a row. Black Sea relay.

MINNIE: Black sea? I wouldn't swim in a black sea.

EDDIE: You must come out covered in tar.

MRS. FRIEDMAN: Ah, to hell with you.

SAM Manetta enters from the pond with a soaking wet KID, coughing.

SAM: You okay?

KID: Yeah.

SAM: What in God's name were you doing out there if you couldn't swim?

KID: I wanted to learn.

SAM: By drowning? Do your parents know where you are?

KID: No.

SAM: They'll be worried sick. Where are you staying?

KID: At Bobbin's.

SAM: All right, get a towel off the line. Dry yourself and I'll take you back.

DORIS: That's Daddy. That's my daddy.

HARRY: Uncle Sam?

DORIS: My daddy. Oh my God, look at him. He was so young. He opened Manetta's in 1936. He was so handsome.

SAM: Hey, you boys, what are you doing over there?

PEEWEE: Nothing.

SAM: Peewee, Harry, get down from there.

HARRY: Hey, look at me, I'm a kid again.

SAM: What's going on up there?

YOUNG HARRY: We're just bird watching, Uncle Sam.

SAM: Bird watching?

PEEWEE: Just some bank swallows.

SAM: Bank swallows, eh?

He climbs to the boys.

Those aren't bank swallows, boys, those are.....

There is a scream.

WOMAN: Ah! Pervert! You should be ashamed of yourself, spying on ladies sunbathing! What are you doing! Give me a towel, Sonya!

SAM: It wasn't me, Mrs. Schulman, it's the boys.

WOMAN: You bring children with you to spy! Shame! *Gay avek! Gay avek!*

SAM: We're going. We're going.... Mrs. Goldman, your tan's coming along very nicely. If you burn, there's vinegar in the kitchen.

WOMAN: Get away!

SAM, YOUNG HARRY, and PEEWEE descend the hill.

SAM: Well, Harry, I hope you boys learned your lesson.

YOUNG HARRY: Oh, we have, Uncle Sam, we really have. See you.

YOUNG HARRY starts to climb the hill again.

SAM: Harry!

DORIS: He was such a mensch, *my daddy. Nothing he wouldn't do for anyone. To see him again. Oh my.*

SAUL from Kensington Market walks by.

SAM: Solly, how are you feeling?

SAUL: Sammy, it's a miracle. My rheumatism's completely gone. My *tuchas* never felt better.

SAM: Watch out for splinters.

SAUL: Your father-in-law is a smart man, building those cottages. Look what's going on now. There's community here. Trotsky would be proud.

SAM: Well, Yukle's a force of nature.

MRS. EICHLER: You gonna pick up the garbage, Mr. Manetta, it's been there since Wednesday?

SAM: As soon as I can, Mrs. Eichler.

MRS. EICHLER: At Lofchick's they pick it up every day.

SAM: Well, next time I'll make you a reservation there. I hear it's very nice. I told you boys to get away from there.

The boys run off.

What am I, a camp counsellor?

MRS. EICHLER: And you tell that Miller boy to leave my Bessie alone. He was supposed to take her for french fries and he took her to the cemetery instead.

SAM: He's not my son, I can't tell him what to do.

MRS. EICHLER: Don't tell me! I'm a guest here, you look after your guests or don't you? I don't need no hanky-panky in the graveyard.

SAM: All right, Mrs. Eichler, I'll tell him.

MRS. EICHLER: And tell your wife to save me the chicken necks. I'll eat them when the kids go to bed.

SAM: All right.

MRS. EICHLER: She's a good cook, your Annie. Like my mother used to make.

MRS. EICHLER exits. MOISHE enters.

MOISHE: Sammy, hang on a minute.

SAM: Hello, Yukle.

MOISHE: You seen that good-for-nothing Harry?

SAM: I saw him a minute ago.

MOISHE: I got a wagon full of firewood he's gotta unload.

SAM: Did you check the house?

MOISHE: You check for me, I don't got time. I'm gonna take a peek at the sunbathers.

He moves to spy on the ladies.

SAM: Yukle.

MOISHE: What?

SAM: They went inside.

MOISHE: Ech. Just my luck. All right. You see that Harry, you give him what for and send him over, it'll be sundown soon.

SAM: All right.

YOUNG DORIS enters. She is fourteen.

YOUNG DORIS: Daddy –

SAM: Doris, you found the Goldbergs' luggage?

YOUNG DORIS: Yah, it was on the back porch.

SAM: What was it doing there?

YOUNG DORIS: Suntanning, I think.

DORIS: Look at that, that's me. She's me.

HARRY: That's you? You weren't that pretty.

DORIS: Shut up, you. Oh my. I used to wear my hair like that. I used to wear barrettes.

HARRY: You were fatter than that.

DORIS: I was slim. I was a living doll. All that running around kept me slim.

HARRY: You remember what you want to remember.

YOUNG DORIS: Daddy, we need wood for tomorrow's weenie roast.

SAM: Your *Zeida* Moishe has lots of wood.

YOUNG DORIS: I need help carrying it.

SAM: I've got to pick up the garbage.

YOUNG DORIS: It's three hours 'til the Sabbath.

SAM: I know, Doris, I know. Did Toronto Packing come?

YOUNG DORIS: Yah.

SAM: And Bernie killed the chickens?

YOUNG DORIS: Yah.

SAM: Your mother's cooking?

YOUNG DORIS: Yah.

SAM: You say anything besides "yah"?

YOUNG DORIS: Yah.

SAM: As long as you're getting a good education. Where's your sister?

YOUNG DORIS: Doing stuff, I don't know.

SAM: And the little one.

YOUNG DORIS: Still taking his nap, I think.

Beat.

SAM: Anything else?

YOUNG DORIS: Mrs. Polsky got a black eye today.

SAM: How?

YOUNG DORIS: The ladies were at Bowin's fighting over fish, and she got hit in the face with a carp.

SAM: Is she all right?

YOUNG DORIS: Yah, but she said next week she's bringing a gun. Oh yah, and at lunch Mrs. Rosenblum said her soup was cold and she sent it back.

SAM: Again?

YOUNG DORIS: Yah. So Mom took it into the kitchen and came back with the same bowl and Mrs. Rosenblum said it was delicious.

SAM: Good. Okay, you find Jackie Miller and tell him to stay away from Bessie Eichler.

YOUNG DORIS: Bessie Eichler makes me vomit. So does Jackie Miller.

SAM: Never mind, Doris, you find him.

YOUNG DORIS: I have to wash dishes.

SAM: You'll wash them later. Please. And meet me in half an hour, we'll get the wood and go meet the train.

YOUNG DORIS: Okay.

SAM: Doris, give me a kiss.

YOUNG DORIS: Daddy.

SAM: A kiss! It gives me energy.

She kisses him.

YOUNG DORIS: Parents dependent on their children's affection have deep psychological problems.

SAM: I'll keep that in mind.

Scene 12: Hair Salon

Two women in a chair waiting, MRS. ISKOWITZ and MRS. BORTS, while MRS. SHLUMPSKY has her hair done by IDA, the hairdresser.

MRS. BORTS: And my Stevie, he does what he wants, he doesn't care. He's wild, like a jackal.

MRS. SHLUMPSKY: *Vus is* (*What is*) a jackal?

MRS. BORTS: A dog, wild like a dog.

IDA: Like a hyena.

MRS. SHLUMPSKY: *Vus hust I gezuk?* (*What did you say?*) Hyena?

IDA: Hyena. It's a wild dog, too.

MRS. SHLUMPSKY: Like a wolf?

MRS. ISKOWITZ: Exactly. A lone wolf.

IDA: Wolves travel in packs.

MRS. ISKOWITZ: What, you work for *National Geographic*? She's telling a story.

ANNIE Manetta enters.

MRS. BORTS: Annie.

DORIS: Mama. Look at her. My mother. She was a beautiful woman.

ANNIE: Hello, Mrs. Borts, how's by you?

MRS. BORTS: Don't ask. My hip. Don't ask. I used to have a figure like you.

ANNIE: (*To hairdresser.*) Ida, I don't have an appointment and I...I see you have people waiting.

MRS. ISKOWITZ: She did me already.

ANNIE: You're done?

MRS. ISKOWITZ: You think I'm this beautiful naturally?

MRS. BORTS: And I'm in no rush, you can go next.

ANNIE: How long will it be, do you think? I have a trainee in the kitchen and I don't want to be away too long.

IDA: Give me five minutes, Mrs. Manetta.

ANNIE: Thank you. (*Beat.*) Is your husband coming up this weekend, Mrs. Iskowitz?

MRS. ISKOWITZ: He's dead.

ANNIE: Dead. Oh, I'm so sorry. I didn't know.

MRS. ISKOWITZ: It's okay. (*Beat.*) It took me two weeks to figure it out. At first I was shocked, but then you get used to it.

MRS. SHLUMPSKY: How's your kids, Mrs. Manetta?

ANNIE: Do I see them? Betty is....who knows. And Doris has decided she wants to be a teacher. Shul is starting to walk.

MRS. SHLUMPSKY: *Zey zolen vaxen hoich vee bamer.* (*They should only grow tall like trees.*)

ANNIE: I like your blouse.

MRS. SHLUMPSKY: Eh?

ANNIE: Your blouse.

MRS. SHLUMPSKY: I don't know where I got it. My mother used to sew all my clothes. Me and my sister.

MRS. ISKOWITZ: Did you hear about Laila Salzburg?

MRS. BORTS: What?

MRS. ISKOWITZ: Her husband left her.

ANNIE: No.

MRS. ISKOWITZ: Yeah. For a teenager.

ANNIE: A teenager?

MRS. ISKOWITZ: Listen, when you're my age, thirty is a teenager. She's taking him to court. She wants the house, the car, everything.

MRS. BORTS: Good luck.

IDA: She'll be lucky to keep her ring.

MRS.SHLUMPSKY: *Ehr iz a mumzer.* (*What a bastard.*)

MRS. BORTS: Like he was the first husband to do such a thing.

MRS. ISKOWITZ: My husband had the decency to die instead.

MRS. BORTS: How's your Sammy?

ANNIE: Good as gold.

MRS. ISKOWITZ: She got a *mensch.* I'm not a people person. I don't even like myself. But your Sammy I like.

ANNIE: Mind you, I don't see him that much. I'm in the kitchen, he's all over the property.

MRS. ISKOWITZ: You got kids, you must see him sometime.

Beat.

ANNIE: The weather should be nice this weekend. Sunshine all Saturday and Sunday. We're full up.

MRS.SHLUMPSKY: You can't get a reservation anywhere. My neighbour went to Nyvelt and she's not even communist.

MRS. BORTS: My apartment in Toronto is impossible. I can't sleep in the summer. It's so hot. In the winter, it's freezing.

SAM Manetta runs in.

SAM: Annie! Hello, ladies. Annie, you should come back.

ANNIE: What's the matter?

SAM: We had a small fire.

ANNIE: What?

SAM: It's okay, it's out, but the trainee –

ANNIE: Elsa.

SAM: She burnt her hand.

ANNIE: Oh my god.

SAM: It's not too bad, but the briskets are ruined.

ANNIE: My briskets.

SAM: Yeah. And the train will be in soon.

ANNIE: Another time, Ida.

IDA: No problem.

ANNIE: Goodbye.

SAM: Goodbye, ladies. You all look gorgeous.

IDA: Bye.

MRS. ISKOWITZ: Bye, Sammy.

MRS. SHLUMPSKY: *All ees gitten.* (*All the best.*)

MRS. BORTS: Take care.

All ladies leave. As they exit:

MRS. ISKOWITZ: Well, I wouldn't kick him out of bed.

This scenes segues into....

Scene 13: Train Station

A CROWD of mostly women and children are milling about talking. Some are holding signs that say White's, Crystal's, Manetta's, Pearlstein's, etc. A train approaches. The crowd goes silent. The train pulls in and men get off. The two groups intersect as a din erupts, families are reunited, and newcomers go off to different cottages.

Scene 14: The Canteen

YOUNG DORIS is there alone, closing up. HARRY and DORIS watch and comment.

DORIS: *I worked at that canteen for seven years. Hot dogs, chips, Pepsi-Cola. We sold everything. Sometimes there'd be a lineup a mile long.*

HARRY: *Not today.*

DORIS: *It's late, I'm just closing up.*

JACKIE Miller arrives on his bike with a few friends.

JACKIE: Give me a Pepsi-Cola.

YOUNG DORIS: I'm closing.

JACKIE: What's your rush, we just got here.

YOUNG DORIS: I have chores at the resort. If you must know.

JACKIE: Your dad owns that dump?

YOUNG DORIS: Manetta's is not a dump, Jackie Miller. It's a high-class resort.

JACKIE: You ain't got a swimming pool like Crystal's.

YOUNG DORIS: We're getting one. Next summer. "Ain't"?

DORIS: *Where did I get that dress?*

JACKIE: You must be your parents' slave, working so hard.

YOUNG DORIS: I'm not a slave, they pay me, for your information.

JACKIE: What do you do with the money?

YOUNG DORIS: I'm saving it.

JACKIE: What for?

YOUNG DORIS: To get out of here. I'm saving for college. You probably don't even know what that is.

JACKIE: Sure, it's where boring people go to die. You still going to be a teacher?

YOUNG DORIS: What do you care?

JACKIE: You'd be a good teacher.

YOUNG DORIS: Why?

JACKIE: You have nice eyes. I'd listen to a teacher with nice eyes.

Beat.

YOUNG DORIS: That… that makes no sense at all – for your information.

JACKIE: Doesn't matter. You still have nice eyes.

Beat.

YOUNG DORIS: I gotta close up.

JACKIE: What are you doing after?

YOUNG DORIS: After what?

JACKIE: After you close.

YOUNG DORIS: Going home. As if it was any of your business.

JACKIE: Thought maybe you'd want to go for french fries.

YOUNG DORIS: It's almost the Sabbath, Jackie.

JACKIE: So? People still do things. We're not in Poland. People do stuff.

YOUNG DORIS: Why do you want to eat french fries with me?

JACKIE: I told you. 'Cause you got nice eyes.

YOUNG DORIS: Well I can't go on *Shabbat.*

JACKIE: Suit yourself.

YOUNG DORIS: But I could go tomorrow. I mean, after sundown. I'll get someone to take my kitchen shift.

JACKIE: Sure, whatever.

YOUNG DORIS: We could meet by Richardson's and go from there.

JACKIE: Okay.

YOUNG DORIS: But I'm not going up to any graveyard.

JACKIE: Who'd wanna go there? Last time Bessie Eichler practically smothered me. I thought she was gonna bury me.

Beat.

YOUNG DORIS: In twenty-five words or less: You ever going to do anything with your life, Jackie Miller?

JACKIE: Sure, I'm gonna be an entre-peneur.

YOUNG DORIS: (*Laughing.*) You have to be able to pronounce it first. It's entre-*preneur*.

JACKIE: Entrepeneur, that's what I said.

YOUNG DORIS: Entre*preneur.*

JACKIE: Entre*preneur.*

YOUNG DORIS: That's it.

JACKIE: I told you you'd be a good teacher. Gotta go.

YOUNG DORIS: I'll see you tomorrow. Sundown. At Richardsons'. We could go to the Sunset Restaurant.

JACKIE: Yeah. See ya. Let's go, guys.

JACKIE and his friends leave.

YOUNG DORIS: That Jackie Miller's going to come to no good. (*Beat.*) But he sure is cute.

Scene 15: Manetta's Resort

ANNIE and SAM, DORIS and HARRY. Music plays.

SAM: Annie, come sit down, it'll be on soon.

ANNIE: I have blintzes on the stove.

YOUNG DORIS: Mom.

SAM: Turn them off, come sit.

ANNIE: All right. Sam, did you get me sugar?

SAM: I'll get it later.

ANNIE: I have cakes to bake.

SAM: I'll get it.

RADIO ANNOUNCER:
Welcome back to the Harry Harris Jewish Hour.

ANNIE: I need sugar.

YOUNG HARRY: Shh. Auntie Annie, it's on.

RADIO ANNOUNCER:
You know, folks, there's nothing like getting out of the city. And there's no place I know that's a better getaway than Manetta's in Pontypool, Ontario. Located between Toronto and Peterborough, it's the perfect escape from the drudgery of the city. But don't take my word for it, listen to this:

RADIO SINGER: (*Sung to a Yiddish melody.*)

Mama wants a little break,
Give her one for heaven's sake
Manetta's has everything required

SAM: Doris.

SAM and DORIS begin to dance. HARRY and ANNIE dance.

RADIO SINGER:

Papa, don't ignore her pleas,
Scrubbing floors down on her knees
A woman works all day until she's tired.
Take a trip where Jewish life is king
Think of all the *nachas* it will bring
Manetta's. Get away from it all.

Scene 16

MOISHE is with MAX, SAM, and ZEV at the still. They have been drinking. YOUNG HARRY is spying on them.

ZEV: In the spring, it floods, I gotta barn that's falling down.

SAM: You want it fixed right, you have to hire someone. Ask Max.

MAX: Sure.

ZEV: What about helping someone out?

MAX: When someone falls in a hole, I help them out.

ZEV: And if *you* fell asleep on the tracks, I'd leave you there!

MAX: At least I wouldn't miss my train. Ha ha. Did you hear?

SAM: What?

MAX: Last night, at three in the morning. The Midnight Flyer stopped!

SAM: It runs through to Montreal.

ZEV: It stopped?

MAX: Did you hear it, Yukle?

MOISHE: I was on it. I was helping Simpson get elected. I missed my train home. Jimmy made a call, got them to stop.

MAX: Jimmy Simpson won?

MOISHE: Mayor of Toronto.

MAX: He's a communist.

ZEV: Socialist.

SAM: Same thing.

ZEV: It's not the same thing.

SAM: Toronto has a socialist mayor, go figure.

MOISHE: He's popular around here.

MAX: Sure, he hates Catholics.

MOISHE: And he doesn't like this Hitler.

MAX: Neither do I.

ZEV: Who do you like?

MAX: I like you – give me a kiss.

ZEV: Get away!

MAX sees YOUNG HARRY.

MAX: Harry, what are you doing there?

YOUNG HARRY: Nothing, Mr. Lofchick.

MOISHE: You're spying?

YOUNG HARRY: I'm looking for worms, to go fishing.

MAX: You want worms, I'll give you worms, tapeworms. Get out of here.

SAM: Harry, go back to the house.

YOUNG HARRY: What are you drinking?

MOISHE: Lemonade. Go home.

YOUNG HARRY: Alcohol is illegal, you know.

ZEV: So is murder, now get out of here.

YOUNG HARRY leaves.

You think that Widow Katznelson will come back this summer? I liked her.

MOISHE: Yeah?

ZEV: If she comes back, I think I've got a shot.

MAX: The best shot you've got is with a gun to your head.

SAM: He's right.

Laughter.

ZEV: Well, I'll live in hope. Ten years my Rachel is gone, it's time for something new.

MOISHE: Eighteen years Hindi's gone..... Where does the time go?

Pause.

SAM: Anyway, it'll be a good summer, gentlemen. Ladies in bathing suits. Think about that.

MOISHE: I like summertime. You can look over your land, see what you've got. In Poland, no one thought I would own a pair of pants, let alone a piece of land, and look.

MAX: More people every summer.

SAM: We're building a swimming pool at Manetta's.

MOISHE: Yeah?

MAX: Crystal's has big entertainment Saturday night.

ZEV: Ach.

SAM: Leo Romberg organizes it.

MAX: He's gonna make a name for himself. Mark my words. (*Beat.*) So many Jews come now, you'd think you were in ancient Israel. We need a synagogue is what we need.

ZEV: What for?

MAX: What for? Saturday services, you *shmendrick.*

ZEV: Ach.

MAX: You got the White's cottages, the Kravitz, Bobbin's, Bernstein, Bornstein, Lofchick's, Pearlstein's, Millers, Badluk.

ZEV: How can they call it that?

MAX: What?

ZEV: Badluk.

SAM: It's their name.

ZEV: Come. Spend the week at Badluck Cottages. Fall in the lake and drown. Get run over by a train.

MOISHE: There's enough hit by trains. On purpose.

ZEV: People have their troubles, Yukle.

MOISHE: I know.

ZEV: Most Jews who come here don't have two nickels to rub together.

MOISHE: So, that's why we offer something reasonable. Good food, accommodation. The town is nice, the people are friendly.

ZEV: Ha ha. Listen to him. They don't care about the town.

MOISHE: What are you talking?

ZEV: The Jews come here to be with their own kind, that's it.

SAM: Zev.

ZEV: Do you march in the Orange Parade? No. They don't want us and we don't want them. Stick with your own kind.

MOISHE: Now you sound like this Hitler.

ZEV: He must be doing something right. Germany's getting stronger.

SAM: The Jews are having a terrible time there.

ZEV: Jews are always having trouble. If people stuck with their own kind, there'd be less trouble.

MAX: Don't you believe in communism, universal brotherhood?

ZEV: Christie Pits in Toronto. Italians and Jews fighting with facists, cracking each other's heads with baseball bats! You have to stick to your own kind. Christians, Blacks, Jews, Chinese. Let them live separate, the way it was intended.

MAX: The eleventh commandment.

SAM: It's getting late.

ZEV: Give me a drink, Yukle.

MOISHE: Go easy. (*Beat.*) The RCMP were sniffing around again. I'm getting lazy. They're gonna catch me.

ZEV: No one's gonna catch you.

MOISHE: What's the charge for making whiskey?

MAX: Twenty years listening to Zev complain.

Laughter.

ZEV: Funny guy.

MOISHE: I've been thinking, boys. It's not an easy decision. I'm going to get rid of the still.

ZEV: What? What are you talking about?

MOISHE: I'm gonna bury it.

ZEV: What if you need it?

MOISHE: I won't.

MAX: Make a map.

MOISHE: Yeah.

MAX: Mail it to the prime minister.

MOISHE: Special delivery.

ZEV: Yukle! People count on you. They come here to take a drink. They look forward to it.

MOISHE: It's a distraction. And it's dangerous.

ZEV: Give it to me.

MOISHE: I'm getting rid of it.

ZEV: I'll keep it safe.

MOISHE: End of story.

Beat.

ZEV: He always has to be the boss. Always the big shot. He used to eat garlic and breathe in people's faces just to get a seat on the bus! Remember? Didn't you come over with nothing, like me?

SAM: Come, Zev, I'll walk you home.

ZEV: What do I got? A little piece of dirt. The soil keeps blowing away. I can't grow nothing. I don't have no hotel or cottages. I ask one little favour, but no! Yukle, the *macher*, does what he wants. He knows all the gentiles, gets the mayor to do him favours.

MAX: Zev, please.

SAM: Come on.

ZEV: For him everything's easy.

MOISHE: I worked, mister. I worked like a dog for my family.

ZEV: I worked, too.

MOISHE: And I made a contribution to this town! Look at this place. Look what it is. Me, Lofchick, Crystal, Sam, we all came here to make a dollar and we made a dollar. Not much, but enough. It's not against the law. Everything I got I earned.

ZEV: I got a barn that's falling down.

MOISHE: And you know what? I'd give it all away. Every penny. Every blessing I ever got, I'd give it all away to have my Hindi back!

SAM: Take it easy.

MOISHE: The rest of the world could go to hell, if I could have her back for five minutes! (*Beat.*) You don't know what you've got. A blessing is to live your life without ever losing a child. Without having a hole in your heart that grows bigger every day. Everything else is honey cake. (*Pause.*) That's it. Time to go. I'm closing down the still.

Scene 17

YOUNG DORIS is dressed up. She stands outside Mr. RICHARDSON's, waiting.

DORIS: *He's not coming. That Jackie Miller. I don't think he ever came to any good.*

HARRY: *You got stood up?*

DORIS: *Someone makes a date with you, it's a date, you don't say you forgot, you don't say you… ah, never mind.*

YOUNG HARRY enters with MARLIE.

HARRY: *Hey, look at that handsome devil. I'm even better looking than I remember. Who's the doll?*

DORIS: *Marlie Shmirler. Your old girlfriend.*

HARRY: *That's Marlie, holy smokes.*

YOUNG HARRY: You got a column for debits and one for credits. So you calculate each month separately and the total…. Hey, what are you doing, Doris?

YOUNG DORIS: Nothing.

MARLIE: Why are you all dressed up?

YOUNG DORIS: It was the Sabbath. I like to dress nice.

YOUNG HARRY: We're going for french fries, want to come?

YOUNG DORIS: No thanks.

YOUNG HARRY: What are you going to do?

YOUNG DORIS: Nothing.

MARLIE: Who are you looking for?

YOUNG DORIS: No one, for your information.

YOUNG HARRY: You're just going to stand here all night?

YOUNG DORIS: What do you care? It's not against the law!

MARLIE: Jeez, we were just trying to be nice.

YOUNG HARRY: We're going to meet up with Fatty Schulman, we could double-date.

YOUNG DORIS: No, thanks.

YOUNG HARRY: He's a nice kid. Fat, but nice.

YOUNG DORIS: Harry, I think I can do better than Fatty Schulman. Go eat your french fries.

MARLIE: I have to be home in an hour.

YOUNG HARRY: All right. See you, Doris.

YOUNG HARRY and MARLIE walk off.

So, you subtract your debits from your credits and what you have left is your monthly balance.

MARLIE: What if you have more debits than credits?

YOUNG HARRY: Well, um… I haven't read that chapter.

YOUNG DORIS says nothing. She looks to see if anyone is coming. She pulls Kleenex tissue out of her bra. Her head droops and she exits.

Interlude 7

DORIS: Why do I remember what I want to forget and forget what I want to remember?

HARRY: Fatty Schulman struck it rich in mayonnaise, you know. Sold it in bulk to restaurants and made a killing.

DORIS: Mayonnaise. Lucky him.

HARRY: He liked you. Always asked about you.

DORIS: Did he marry?

HARRY: No. He had a coronary at thirty-five, you could have been a rich widow.

DORIS: You always look on the bright side, Harry.

HARRY: I'm an optimist.

Scene 18: Crystal's Hotel, Saturday night

ANNOUNCER: Ladies and Gentleman, *mishpochas* and *meshuganahs!* Crystal's Resort is proud to present, direct from downtown Toronto, the man who puts onions in your herring and the kish in your *kishka*, the irreverent, the impertinent, Louie Weingarten!

LOUIE (*aka Johnny Wayne*):
Thank you, thank you, it's great to be back in Pontypool. Where else can you take a vacation that makes you wish you were back in Toronto? No, seriously, I love it here. The only place you can find three rabbis on the beach, eating chopped liver from ice cream cones. It looks like chocolate, but with a few fried onions. No really, Pontypool's a great town, the gentiles welcome us with open arms. Or they're reminding us that we killed their saviour. In any case, the important thing is that we show mutual respect. They ignore us and we ignore them. And now on the occasion of Harvey and Sheila Blitzstein's fiftieth wedding anniversary, I'd just like to say – Kids, are you sure you're ready to make a commitment? There's still time. Hit it, Rudy!

Piano music plays.

(*Sings.*)

Mrs. Schwartz lost her shorts
Found them in a pot of *borscht*

Oy oy oy a mechia.

Mr. Mandel lit a candle
Melted down and burnt his sandals
Now he stays awake in case of fire.

Everybody has a little quirk
I make fun of them 'cause that's my work.

Oy oy oy a mechia.

The Shermans are a gloomy lot
Mr. Sherman bought a plot
Put Mrs. Sherman in without permission

Yacov took some strudel dough
Put the whole thing up his nose
Then sneezed it out and made some nice *knishes*

Everybody's got a little quirk
I make fun of them 'cause I'm a jerk

Oy oy oy a mechia.

Botkin, Bergel, Cohen
All want to play French horn
And wish like Benny Goodman they were stars

But Leo Romberg's very wise
He says the stars are in their eyes
And in showbiz they'll only get *Shofar*
(*Shofar*, sho good, you know what I'm shaying.)

It's true that good things come to those who wait
So *maideleh* go pick up the fish plates

Oy oy oy a mechia.

You can stay at White's or Pearlstein's,
But please don't touch the girl-steins
They will only date *Lubovitch* boys

At Crystal's they're not picky
Shayna maidel had a hickey
And I heard she got it from a local *goy*.

Enter HERSCHEL, breathless.

HERSCHEL: Stop the music, stop the music!

LOUIE: Hey kid, audience participation's in the next act. Now if you'll excuse –

HERSCHEL: He's dead, he's dead!

LOUIE: Who's dead, kid?

HERSCHEL: Mr. Bernstein. Moishe Yukle Bernstein is dead.

Beat.

LOUIE: *Oy vay.*

End of Act One.

Moishe (Dov Mickelson) and Constable Niles (Matt Gilbert) discuss immigration policy.

Jews being separated upon arrival in Treblinka, Poland. (Ensemble)

ACT TWO
Scene 1: Train Station, 1942

Empty platform. A train approaches. A large group of men, women, and children alight. They hold suitcases and packs. A general din erupts. Suddenly a Nazi OFFICER and SS men with machine guns emerge.

OFFICER: *Achtung Juden!*

The crowd goes silent.

Juden aufgepasst! Ihr seid hier in Treblinka. Lasst euer Gepäck und eure anderen Sachen hier auf einem Haufen. Die kriegt ihr später. Ihr bekommt jetzt Duschen und einen Platz zum Schlafen. Frauen und Kinder nach links, Männer nach rechts. Jetzt sofort. Schnell, schnell, schnell!

(Attention Jews! You are in Treblinka. Put your luggage and possessions in a pile here. You will get them later. You will receive showers and a place to sleep. Women and children to the left, men to the right. Now. Fast, fast, fast!)

Two signs are held up. One says "Frauen und Kinder," the other says "Männer." The train pulls out of the station as the two separated lines are marched off by the soldiers.

Scene 2: Manetta's

ANNIE, SAM, YOUNG DORIS, YOUNG HARRY, and some guests sit around a crackling radio.

RADIO REPORTER: Details are just becoming available. I'd like to say this to you, Canada. We have suffered heavy losses and I saw our men die, but never have I seen men die more bravely or with such great heart as our Canadian troops. The word "Dieppe" may rank with Vimy Ridge in our history. And our hats are off to the Royal Canadian Engineers and the Royal Canadian Army Medical Corps. And the South Saskatchewan Regiment, and the Queen's Own Cameron Highlanders of Winnipeg, and the Royal Regiment from Toronto, and the Essex Scottish from Windsor, and the Royal Hamilton Light Infantry, and Les Fusiliers de Montréal. A lot of those men will never return to Canada and many may not return until after the war, if the German count of fifteen hundred prisoners is correct. It's a sad day for Canada, but one that.....

SAM turns off the radio. Silence.

MR. SOLOMON: My nephew is in the Essex Scottish. Oh my god. It's a slaughter.

MR. SHERMAN: Goddamn Krauts. They're animals.

SAM: Maybe your nephew is fine.

MR. SOLOMON: From your mouth to God's ears.

Pause.

ANNIE: More tea?

Pause.

MR. SOLOMON: I'm going for a walk. The fresh air will do me good.

MR. SHERMAN: I'll keep you company.

They exit.

SAM: It's a national disaster.

ANNIE: Canada used to feel so safe.

YOUNG DORIS: Were they all Canadian soldiers?

YOUNG HARRY: Canadians are the best-trained allied force in Europe. This is a minor setback.

SAM approaches ANNIE and puts his arms around her. They begin to sway.

SAM: I'll keep you safe, Annie, with every fibre of my being, I'll keep you safe.

They kiss and continue swaying. DORIS and HARRY watch.

Scene 3

JD THOMAS addresses a crowd.

JD THOMAS: And I say to you that the land under your feet will blow away if we don't do something. The soil is weak, full of sand hummocks, gullies of clay, and if we don't address it now, this entire region will become a dust bowl. Water will disappear and our communities will die.

MAN 1: How you gonna save my fields, Mr. Thomas?

JD THOMAS: The Ganaraska Watershed will reverse soil erosion, improve water retention, and increase the land's fertility throughout the entire moraine.

FARMER: I had a bumper crop two years ago, now I can't grow nothing.

JD THOMAS: Well, you see….

WOMAN 1: I can't feed my family.

WOMAN 2: I got three babies at home.

JD THOMAS: Now, hang on. Hang on. Our aim is to plant two million trees and create a watershed that ensures the viability of our communities for the next thousand years. It will create hundreds of jobs, fertile land, clean, plentiful water and a healthy future for all Ontarians.

SAMMY CRYSTAL: Mr. Thomas, Sammy Crystal from the *Telegram*. This Ganaraska project sounds pretty ambitious, how long's it gonna take?

JD THOMAS: Well, with your help, in just a few short years, we can make this land the envy of the world. If we work together…

The crowd grumbles.

Now, now, settle down. I have some brochures.

MAN 1: This is a waste of time, I'm going.

MAN 2: Can I get a ride with you to Lindsay?

MAN 1: Sure.

WOMAN 3: You better go now. The train gets in soon, you'll be stuck here for at least an hour.

MAN 2: Why?

WOMAN 3: All the Jews will be at the station. You won't be able to drive anywhere.

MAN 1: You can't even walk on the street it's so busy. In Europe they keep 'em in ghettoes.

WOMAN 3: Well, the town makes a nice living off them coming up here.

MAN 1: You got all these rabbis walking around like they own the place.

WOMAN 3: How do you know they're rabbis?

MAN 1: They got beards, don't they?

MAN 2: Yeah, and if you hit one with your car, they sue you two minutes later.

They laugh. SAM arrives. He listens unseen.

WOMAN 3: Well, I've rented out my extra room and I've never had any complaints. They're very respectful.

MAN 1: All right.

WOMAN 3: This town would be dead quiet without them.

MAN 1: Well, come the Sabbath a little peace and quiet is all I want.

SAM: Mrs. Jarvis, how are you?

WOMAN 3: Fine, Mr. Manetta, just fine.

SAM: I was wondering if you've got any space this week. I'm overbooked and I need a room for two.

WOMAN 3: It just so happens I do, Mr. Manetta.

SAM: They're a religious couple, but they shouldn't be any trouble.

WOMAN 3: That's fine, everyone can have their God as far as I'm concerned.

SAM: And since it's last-minute, they're willing to pay four dollars a night instead of three. Is that all right?

WOMAN 3: That's fine, Mr. Manetta, very generous.

MAN 1: I got an extra room at my place. It needs a little work but…

MAN 2: I got a shed I could fix up. It's pretty cozy.

WOMAN 3: Get in line, gentlemen, get in line.

SAM: I'll bring them by about 2:00?

WOMAN 3: I'll be there, see you then.

SAM: Bye-bye.

WOMAN 3 starts to go as the men follow her.

MAN 1: You tell him I got a place, Marge, I'll fix it up this week.

MAN 2: My place is pretty much ready.

MAN 1: Hang on, I'm talking to her. Marge…?

They exit.

Scene 4: The Wedding

Manetta's Resort. Guests assemble for a wedding. A wedding OFFICIANT waits. Music plays. The GROOM enters, stands at the front. "Do Di Li" plays as the BRIDE enters wearing a veil. She walks to the front. Under the chupah.

OFFICIANT: I would like to welcome all of our guests here today, the families and friends of the happy couple, and many thanks to our hosts for the lovely preparations. It gives me great pleasure to bring these two wonderful people together and to set them on the road to a happy life. The *Ketubah* has been written, the *chupah* erected and all that awaits is their sworn love for each other. Do you, Herschel Ephraim Cooperman, take Brenda Esther Slabotsky to be your wedded wife, to love and honour according to the laws of Moses and Israel?

HERSCHEL: I do.

OFFICIANT: And do you, Brenda Esther Slabotsky, take Herschel Ephraim Cooperman to be your husband, to love and honour according to the laws of Moses and Israel?

BRIDE nods her head.

With the power invested in me by the province of Ontario and the Levitt Salami company, I now pronounce you man and wife.

HERSCHEL breaks a glass. The people cheer.

You may kiss the bride.

The BRIDE removes her veil and we see that she is, in fact, a man. The couple kiss and the BRIDE sweeps the GROOM into her arms and runs off with him. The crowd goes

Sam (Jordan Kanner), Annie (Marie Jones), Young Doris (Caitlin Driscoll), and Young Harry (Griffin Clark) hear news of the tragedy at Dieppe.

An old Russian Jewish Wedding Dance. (Ensemble)

crazy and breaks into a Hora folk dance, with Russian Kazatska flourishes. YOUNG DORIS is front and centre; someone lifts her onto his shoulders and she begins to laugh ecstatically, having the time of her life.

Interlude 1

DORIS: Sometimes it was important to be foolish, just to be foolish. The world had enough problems. Here we could escape our troubles and pretend everything was alright.

HARRY: You can only hide from life for so long.

Scene 5: The Swing Inn, 1948

Music plays on a jukebox. Kids dance.

YOUNG DORIS and MARLIE, sipping Cokes.

MARLIE: He's cute.

YOUNG DORIS: Who?

MARLIE: In the blue shirt.

YOUNG DORIS: He looks like trouble.

MARLIE: You say that about everyone, Doris.

YOUNG DORIS: They're boys, Marlie, what do you expect.

MARLIE: When was the last time you had a date, Doris? When?

YOUNG DORIS: With Herbie Allen, for your information.

MARLIE: You mean the Dominion Day dance? That was in Grade Eight.

YOUNG DORIS: So.

MARLIE: That's four years ago.

YOUNG DORIS: Forget it. (*Beat.*) Where's Harry?

MARLIE: I'm finished with him. All he wants to do is talk about balancing books.

YOUNG DORIS: He wants to be an accountant.

MARLIE: Yeah, well, he can count me out. I want to dance.

YOUNG DORIS: Go ahead.

MARLIE: Dance with me.

YOUNG DORIS: I don't feel like it.

MARLIE: You're a lot of fun. Who's that?

YOUNG DORIS: Where?

MARLIE: There.

YOUNG DORIS: I don't know.

MARLIE: He's looking at you.

YOUNG DORIS: Maybe he's cross-eyed.

MARLIE: He's coming over. No, he stopped. No, he's coming. If he asks you to dance, you have to.

YOUNG DORIS: Shut up.

MARLIE: You have to.

YOUNG DORIS: Shut up.

The boy (MARTIN) approaches.

MARTIN: Hey, Doris. Remember me?

YOUNG DORIS: No.

MARTIN: Martin Applebaum.

YOUNG DORIS: No.

MARTIN: My family stayed at Manetta's two summers ago.

YOUNG DORIS: Oh, right. You burnt off your eyebrows at the bonfire.

MARTIN: Yeah. They grew back, though.

YOUNG DORIS: Didn't you wear corrective shoes?

MARTIN: They worked.

YOUNG DORIS: You look taller.

MARTIN: Yeah, I guess I grew. (*To MARLIE.*) I'm Martin.

MARLIE: Marlie. Hi.

MARTIN: Hi. Great jukebox.

MARLIE: Only one in town. You ever been to the Swing Inn before?

MARTIN: Nah. I was too young. Only the big kids came here.

MARLIE: Now we're the big kids.

MARTIN: Yeah.

Beat.

MARLIE: Where are you staying?

MARTIN: Me? Oh, in a field tent with my company. I'm working this summer.

YOUNG DORIS: The Ganaraska Watershed?

MARTIN: Yeah.

MARLIE: Must be hard.

MARTIN: I figure I planted five thousand trees in the last six weeks.

MARLIE: Wow. Must build a lot of muscle.

MARTIN: Yeah. I guess.

MARLIE: You must get pretty dirty.

MARTIN: Yeah.

YOUNG DORIS: You don't have showers?

MARTIN: There's one in the camp, but it's freezing.

YOUNG DORIS: Manetta's has a pool now. If you want, after work you could come for a swim. I do lifeguarding on Thursdays, Saturdays, and Sundays.

MARTIN: Yeah, that sounds good. I haven't been swimming in a long – (*The music changes to "Everybody Loves Somebody Sometime."*) Oh man, I love this song.

MARLIE: It's Dean Martin.

MARTIN: Same name as me.

YOUNG DORIS: What a coincidence.

MARTIN: You wanna dance?

Beat.

MARLIE: Who? Me?

MARTIN: Yeah.

MARLIE: Is it okay, Doris?

YOUNG DORIS: I'm not your mother, I don't care.

MARLIE: You sure?

YOUNG DORIS: Go ahead.

MARLIE: Okay. Let's go.

MARTIN: Nice seeing you, Doris. I might come by for that swim.

MARLIE and MARTIN go off to dance.

YOUNG DORIS: I won't hold my breath.

The music plays. The kids dance. DORIS sits down and sips her Coke.

I hate this stupid town.

Interlude 2

HARRY: Growing up is a heartache.

DORIS: You get used to it. Anyway, believe me, I had plenty of dates later, for your information.

HARRY: Yeah?

DORIS: I did, Harry.

HARRY: You ever go out with Benny Farber?

DORIS: Benny Farber only had one eye.

HARRY: That's why they called him a good looker. I wonder if that Marlie's still single, she was a hot tamale.

DORIS: She married a boy from Etobicoke. Frozen foods.

HARRY: He could have died. I should look her up. (*Beat.*) Ah, Doris. Doris! Look at me. You were beautiful then and you're beautiful now.

DORIS: You silly goose. (*Beat.*) I was pretty, wasn't I?

HARRY: Sure.

DORIS: Ah. Youth is wasted on the young. (*She pulls Kleenex tissues out of her brassier and looks at them.*) I spent so much time thinking I didn't fit in.

HARRY: Sure, you did. Sure. Just don't tell anyone I said that, it'll cramp my style.

DORIS: Anyway, I had no time for boys. My parents needed help. And I was saving for teachers' college.

HARRY: Where were your brother and sister?

DORIS: They were busy. (*To audience.*) It was the fifties, it was a new era. Moishe and Rifka were gone, but the war was finally over, there was hope in the world, the Jews had a country, Pontypool was booming. We even built a synagogue.

Scene 6: Opening of Pontypool Synagogue, Rosh Hashanah

RABBI: *Tekki-ah.* (*The* Shofar, *a ram's horn, is blown.*)

Baruch atah Adonai Eloheinu Melech Ha'Olam, asher kidishanu b'mitzvotav v'tzivanu leshoma kol shofar.

CROWD: Amen. Blessed are You, Lord our God, King of the Universe, who has blessed us in his commandments and commanded us to hear the sound of the *shofar.*

RABBI: *Baruch atah Adonai Eloheinu Melech Ha'Olam, shehechiyanu v'kiyimanu v'higianu la'zman ha'zeh.*

CROWD: Amen. Blessed are You, Lord our God, King of the Universe, who has kept us alive, sustained us, and brought us to this season.

CROWD: (*To one another.*) *Y'asher ko-ach.*

RABBI: Dear friends. At this *Rosh Hashanah* festival we blow the *shofar* to sound in the New Year and to ask God's blessings. But the *shofar* is more than just a trumpet. It is the breath of the Almighty Himself. It stirs the recesses of our conscience and ignites our inner passion. It reminds us of the ram Abraham sacrificed *instead* of his son Isaac. It reminds us of the destruction of the Temple *and* its rebuilding. And finally, it proclaims the time when the exiled can return to the promised land and God's reign of righteousness can begin.

We have now, *Hashem* be blessed, Israel, a country where Jews can thrive, where those who suffered the atrocities of war can heal and create new generations. We have a state that can be a light to all the nations. And here in Pontypool, we finally have, *Hashem* be blessed, our own synagogue.

The congregation breaks into applause and cheering: "Mazel Tov!" "A zei gezunt!"

That miracle came to pass, thanks to the good people of this community. I hope the coming years will fill this house with questions and learning, with *mitzvoth* and mirth. And finally, I am pleased to announce, at the conclusion of this service, Sam and Annie Manetta have invited the congregation to their resort for a *Kiddush.* A little *schnapps,* a little apple cake and maybe even a piece of Annie's *gefilte* fish, God willing, if Sammy didn't eat it all. And now to conclude our service, please join in the singing of *Adon Olam*.

Congregation sings "Adon Olam" ("Master of the Universe") and slowly exits.

Adon olam, asher malach, b'terem kol y'tzir nivra.
L'et na'asah v'cheftzo kol, azai melech sh'mo nikra.
V'acharey kichlot hakol, l'vado yimloch nora.
V'hu haya, v'hu hoveh, v'hu yih'yeh b'tifara.
V'hu echad, v'eyn sheni l' hamshil lo, l'hachbira.
B'li reishit, b'li tachlit, v'lo ha'oz v'hamisrah.
V'hu Eli, v'chai go'ali, v'tzur chevli b'et tzarah.
V'hu nisi umanos li, m'nat kosi b'yom ekra.

YOUNG DORIS: To him I commit my spirit, in the time of sleep and awakening, even if my spirit leaves, God is with me, I shall not fear.

Interlude 3

DORIS: That synagogue. It was the height of Jewish life in Pontypool. The people kept coming, and their children would come. And new immigrants from Europe that survived the war. They found a home there, too. I remember, 1953, I'll never forget, I was working as a lifeguard.

Scene 7: The Pool

People swimming, sunbathing.

Young DORIS as a lifeguard blows a whistle at kids in the pool.

YOUNG DORIS: Shlomo! No splashing. No more warnings.

SHLOMO: It's Aaron, not me.

YOUNG DORIS: I'll ban you both from the pool.

SHLOMO: It's Aaron. Aaron, stop it.

AARON: Stop what? I'm not doing anything.

MRS. FRIEDMAN (from earlier) walks by, standing straight. EDDIE and MINNIE appear.

EDDIE: Mrs. Friedman, race me again. I'll beat you this time.

MRS. FRIEDMAN: No.

MINNIE: You have to, Mrs. Friedman.

MRS. FRIEDMAN: I beat him fair and square, Odessa city champion.

EDDIE: Best two out of three.

MRS. FRIEDMAN: Go play tiddlywinks.

EDDIE: You can't tell anyone you beat me, you can't.

MINNIE: You can't, Mrs. Friedman.

MRS. FRIEDMAN: Ah, shaddap.

YOUNG DORIS: Mrs. Boravsky.

MRS. BORAVSKY: Eh?

YOUNG DORIS: Is that yours?

MRS. BORAVSKY: My what?

YOUNG DORIS: You dropped something.

MRS. BORAVSKY: Oh. My noodle *kugel.*

MR. KAPNER: I'll get it for you. (*He picks it up.*)

MRS. BORAVSKY: I was going to have it for lunch.

MR. KAPNER: It's just got a little grass on it, good as new.

MRS. BORAVSKY: It's got sand. I can't eat that.

MR. KAPNER: I ate worse things, believe me. Bugs, rats. Potato peelings when I was lucky.

Beat.

MRS. BORAVSKY: Where were you?

MR. KAPNER: All over. First Chelmno, then Buchenwald. I was liberated from Auschwitz. I went back to Lodz after the war, but my *shtetl* was gone. Nothing left. Not even a gravestone.

MRS. BORAVSKY: I lived in Lodz when I was a girl. Then we moved.

MR. KAPNER: So I came here 1949. Almost went to Israel, but I knew a little English so I came here. With nothing. I had my fingers, at least, I could still sew.

MRS. BORAVSKY: We got out 1940. Forged papers, through Holland.

MR. KAPNER: Then you have a charmed life.

Beat.

MRS. BORAVSKY: What's your name?

MR. KAPNER: Kapner. Eddie Kapner. Pleased to meet you… Mrs.?

Beat.

MRS. BORAVSKY: Edel Kapner?

MR. KAPNER: Yes, you are?

MRS. BORAVSKY: Edel Kapner from Lodz?

MR. KAPNER: Yes.

MRS. BORAVSKY: I lived in Lodz. In the Kutno *shtetl.*

MR. KAPNER: I'm from Kutno.

MRS. BORAVSKY: I knew your mother, Mindel Kapner. She used to make special –

MR. KAPNER and MRS. BORAVSKY: – Braided *challahs…*

MRS. BORAVSKY: For the holidays. For the whole village. She was a wonderful baker. (*Beat.*) Manya Boravsky. I knew your mother. I knew her. Is she still…?

MR. KAPNER: Gone. (*Beat.*) My brothers, sisters, everyone. I was lucky, I got a number. Who'd think getting a number would be lucky.

MRS. BORAVSKY: Come, Edel. (*Beat.*) Come eat some *kugel.* We'll talk about home.

Interlude 4

HARRY: The first time I saw someone with tattooed numbers, I thought he was an accountant. No joke.

DORIS: There were a lot of survivors in the fifties. I remember they were very quiet and their eyes were all sunken. If the police ever came by, they would run and hide in their rooms.

HARRY: But every once in a while, two old souls were reunited. Pontypool wasn't much, but compared to Europe, it was Shangri-La.

Scene 8: Manetta's Resort, end of the season

The final duck luncheon of the summer.

SAM, ANNIE, and Young DORIS Manetta are talking to patrons as they leave the tables and gather their suitcases for the journey home.

MR. ROSENBLUM: Annie. Just terrific. I never had duck like that. Just terrific.

ANNIE: Thank you, Mr. Rosenblum. It was our pleasure.

MR. ROSENBLUM: I'm stuffed, maybe I'll take a nap in the kitchen.

MRS. ROSENBLUM: You have to give me the recipe.

SAM: It's a secret, she won't even tell me.

YOUNG DORIS: She just uses *kosher* ducks.

MR. ROSENBLUM: *Kosher* ducks? You mean you *slit their throats and let all the blood drip out*?

MRS. ROSENBLUM: Morris, you'll frighten Doris.

MR. ROSENBLUM: Nah, kids like gross things, don't you, Doris?

YOUNG DORIS: I like you, Mr. Rosenblum.

SAM: You have all your luggage?

MR. ROSENBLUM: Sure. We got everything. It's not a long drive.

SAM: Well, I hope we'll see you next summer. It's always a pleasure having you.

Beat.

MRS. ROSENBLUM: You didn't tell them?

MR. ROSENBLUM: I was going to.

SAM: What?

MR. ROSENBLUM: My brother, Solly. You know him. He used to come up here.

ANNIE: I remember him.

SAM: Sure, with the rheumatism.

YOUNG DORIS: He used to pick his nose at the table.

SAM: Doris!

YOUNG DORIS: Well, he did.

MR. ROSENBLUM: He didn't read Emily Post. Anyway, he bought some land up in Haliburton this summer.

SAM: Haliburton?

MRS. ROSENBLUM: Sure. A lot of Jews are buying up there.

MR. ROSENBLUM: Muskoka, too.

ANNIE: What's there?

MR. ROSENBLUM: Are you kidding? They got more lakes than they know what to do with. Not like the *ferkakta* pond we got here. You can't wash your socks in it without causing a drought. Anyway, he's building a cottage. He made good money during the war, selling boots to the army.

MRS. ROSENBLUM: He's building a *big* cottage. So next year, we're going up there.

ANNIE: It's so far from Toronto.

MR. ROSENBLUM: They're gonna put in a new road. You can zip up there in no time.

MRS. ROSENBLUM: Well, I always had a nice time here. I'll miss this place.

MR. ROSENBLUM: I'll miss Annie's cooking.

ANNIE: We'll miss you, too. Have a safe trip home.

MR. ROSENBLUM: Look after yourself, Doris. Don't take any wooden nickels.

YOUNG DORIS: Thanks for the advice.

MRS. ROSENBLUM: Doris, you got a boyfriend yet?

YOUNG DORIS: Yeah, his brother Solly. We pick our noses together.

SAM: Doris!

MR. ROSENBLUM: Well, see you around.

ANNIE and SAM: Goodbye.

MR. and MRS. ROSENBLUM leave.

SAM: Muskoka.

ANNIE: It's too far, it'll never catch on.

The TEITLEMANS and their kids approach.

IRA: Sammy boy, thanks for all the onions.

SAM: Always nice to have you, Ira. We'll see you next summer?

IRA: Wouldn't miss it for the world.

ANNIE: David, Joel, did you have a good time?

DAVID: Yes, thank you.

JOEL: Yes, thank you.

SAM: Next summer we're going to have kids' entertainment, too. A magician. A juggler. Would you like that?

DAVID: Yes, thank you.

JOEL: Yes, thank you.

IRA: They're going to have to miss that. They're going to camp.

DAVID: I don't want to go to camp.

IRA: Never mind, it's good for you.

ANNIE: What camp?

IRA: They're building a summer camp. Near Tweed. Camp Gesher.

YOUNG DORIS: Tweed? Where's that?

IRA: I don't know. They'll take them on a bus.

ANNIE: There's lots of kids here. What do they need to go to camp for?

IRA: It's a Zionist camp. It helps build Israel. We've got a country now, we've got to do our part to support it, no?

SAM: Sure.

IRA: Nobody likes the Jews. If we have to fight another war, they're going to need our help, you know.

SAM: Of course.

IRA: Come on, kids. We'll get some Mello-Rolls on the way home.

DAVID: I don't like Mello-Rolls.

JOEL: I don't like Mello-Rolls.

IRA: Well, I like them. Let's go. *Anachnu holchim achshav.* (*We have to go.*)

The TEITLEMANS exit.

YOUNG DORIS: Tweed? Who'd want to go to Tweed? Sounds worse than Pontypool.

ANNIE: Goodbye, Mrs. Frumstein, don't forget your shawl.

SAM: See you, Lonny.

ANNIE: Look after yourself, Sharon.

SAM: Keep up that diet, you look great.

ANNIE: Thanks for coming.

SAM: Safe trip. Bye.

ANNIE: Bye. See you next summer.

YOUNG DORIS: Bye.

Everyone has gone.

SAM: Well. That's that. I'm gonna pick up the garbage. I'll see you in a bit.

SAM leaves.

ANNIE: I'm going to make sure they don't pack the meat and milk dishes together. You could start with the linens, Doris. (*Beat.*) Doris?

YOUNG DORIS: Mama, are we going to stay here forever?

ANNIE: What do you mean?

YOUNG DORIS: Just this, over and over for the rest of our lives.

ANNIE: You can do anything you want to do, Doris.

YOUNG DORIS: But do I have to do it here?

ANNIE: No, you can go someplace else, I suppose. To study, you mean?

YOUNG DORIS: To be a teacher. That's what I'm saving for.

ANNIE: I know. I wanted to be a teacher too, once upon a time. Your *Zeida* Moishe used to tell me, "Girls don't need to go to school because it makes men nervous." So I ended up here. Back then it was a different world. Today you can be whatever you want. (*Beat.*) You live the way you want to live, Doris, and don't let any man ever tell you different.

YOUNG DORIS: All right, Mama.

They hug.

Thank you, Mama.

ANNIE: You're welcome.

Interlude 5

DORIS: I had to think about my future. I couldn't spend my whole life in Pontypool. Stupid town. It was nowhere. If I wanted to be a teacher, I had to live, see the world.

HARRY: So where did you go?

DORIS: Toronto. Like everyone else. And Pontypool was changing. They still came in the summer, but fewer and fewer.

HARRY: The Jews were doing better. Making money, running businesses. They were buying cottages, building other resorts. Pontypool was turning back into the sleepy town it used to be.

Scene 9: The Bank

MR. CALLAGHAN looks at some figures on a paper.

MR.CALLAGHAN: I'm sorry, Sam, but that's the prognosis.

SAM: Do it again.

MR.CALLAGHAN: The numbers won't change. I did it three times. You're not making enough.

SAM: But if we –

MR.CALLAGHAN: You've got to pay your suppliers, Sam, your loan interest. Your bookings are down. You're not making a profit, how can you stay in business?

SAM: We're going to do more advertising.

MR.CALLAGHAN: The resort's not even half full. Things are changing. The train doesn't come here anymore.

SAM: I have a family, Donald.

MR.CALLAGHAN: Look, I call it as I see it. The resort industry had its day here. People find other ways to spend their money. They take trips on airplanes, they buy new modern cottages. Look, Sam, your people have done well for themselves. They sewed their way into better neighbourhoods, better schools and now better vacations. What's Pontypool got on the Catskills or California? You make money, you want to spend it someplace special. Pontypool is a little ordinary.

SAM: I put a fortune into that resort. The pool, the dining room, the –

MR. CALLAGHAN: Sam. I'm sorry. I can't guarantee loans to Manetta's anymore. Crystal's is closed now, Lofchick's, Badluk. And the cottages I've seen lately are in terrible shape. People want modern conveniences.

Beat.

SAM: I'm bleeding money. I couldn't pay the kitchen staff last week. I'll lose the property without a miracle.

MR. CALLAGHAN: You got anything socked away?

SAM: No. I'm busted.

MR. CALLAGHAN: You got a nice property there, Sammy. A lot of trees. You could do something with those. It might tide you over for a bit.

SAM: Yeah. Thanks for your help, Mr. Callaghan. You've always been a decent guy and I appreciate it. Thanks for the help.

MR. CALLAGHAN: Wish I could do more, Sam. It's not just you that's suffering, it's the whole town.

SAM: Yeah, well... I don't have to feed the whole town.

Scene 10

Young DORIS enters alone with a suitcase. She looks around.

YOUNG DORIS: Goodbye, stupid town. I won't miss you. And I won't forget you. (*Beat.*) Thanks for all the lousy memories. Working endless hours for a pittance, having to always be polite, never having any privacy. (*Beat.*) There's not even a stupid train out of here, I have to get a bus. Ach. (*Beat.*) Well, stupid town. I guess this is it. The next time you see me, I'll be a different person. Don't miss me too much.

Young DORIS leaves.

Interlude 6

DORIS: My leaving was the nail in the coffin. The resort had been a labour of love for my parents. And now it was unsustainable.

HARRY: Everyone was leaving. It was like the exodus all over again. Once there were crowds like you'd never seen, now it was dwindling to nothing. Businesses were selling out for a song.

DORIS: Daddy was in dire straits. So desperate times called for desperate measures. What's a poor Jew with nothing but a few pine trees going to do to make a living?

Scene 11: Manetta Home

ANNIE: Christmas trees?

SAM: I've sold two hundred so far. It'll help us through the winter.

ANNIE: You're selling Christmas trees?

SAM: Yeah.

ANNIE: It's not good for the soil, Sam, chopping down all those trees. The whole Ganaraska –

SAM: Annie, don't start with Ganaraska. They planted two million trees, I can sell a few – on my own land – to put food on the table.

ANNIE: A Jew selling Christmas trees?

SAM: Jesus was Jewish, it makes sense. Quebec, Chicago, Boston, Detroit, they all want them.

ANNIE: And what then, when the trees are gone?

SAM: We'll plant some more. We have to survive, Annie. Everything we had, we put into the resort. We need to start again. Or we'll lose the property.

ANNIE: This isn't the future I was planning.

SAM: I didn't win the Irish sweepstakes, all right! I'm a hard-working nobody, who never caught a break.

ANNIE: I didn't mean it like that.

SAM: It doesn't matter.

ANNIE: Sam.

SAM: What can we do? We'll sell Christmas trees. And later we'll worry about later. I still have mouths to feed and I'll do it with Christmas trees if that's the way it has to be. If I have to, I'll dress up as Santa Claus.

Interlude 7

DORIS: And he sold Christmas trees and made enough to survive. For a while. He even patented a machine to wrap the trees so the branches didn't break. He was a smart man, my daddy. Maybe not lucky, but smart. He knew how to pinch a nickel into a dime when he had to. And when Mama died, my mother… well, everything changed. The resort fell into disrepair and eventually….disappeared. Later, Daddy remarried, but I was teaching in Toronto, and Pontypool was a distant memory to me.

HARRY: It was another era. My accountant phase. When you could use a little spit to polish a bus token and sell it for your supper. Now everything's different. Now everyone lives on credit and the day you die is the first day you're free. That's why I always carry a high balance on my Visa, so when I drop dead, I can really stick it to those *mumzers*.

DORIS: Anyway. It was a life, anyway. Some of it I remember good, a little I make up. To fill in the gaps.

HARRY: Ah. What's memory, anyway? It's overrated. When you remember, it's like you're making it up anyway. It doesn't really exist. Like us, we won't exist one day. Think of all the other stories of Pontypool, where are they? And them, all of them. One day they'll all be gone too. We're passing through our lives. Like people passed through Pontypool. A river flows, the land comes to life. The river dries, the land goes to sleep. That's how it's always been.

DORIS: I met so many people there, so many friends. Where are they now?

HARRY: Florida. Dead. The usual. See, I don't live in the past. I live for the moment. I'd rather have a good smoked meat sandwich today than remember one I had thirty years ago.

DORIS: Good smoked meat, in Toronto?

HARRY: All right, I'm a bit of a dreamer, but you get my point.

DORIS: Look, they were all dreamers. All those people who came here, with no money, no language. If they'd stayed back in the old country, they wouldn't have survived. We wouldn't know their stories. Pontypool, it's magic, this place was pure magic.

Scene 12: Pontypool Reunion, 2005

People are arriving and meeting.

VOICE 1: *Millie, is that you? Millie Caplan. It's Essie Abrams.*

VOICE 2: *Oh my God. You look exactly the same.*

VOICE 3: *We used to vacation, just over there. Go see movies in the Orange Hall.*

VOICE 4: *My oh my, it's changed so much.*

VOICE 5: *I remember you. You were this tall when I saw you, last. Just a* pitzikle.

VOICE 6: *This is my daughter Rachel. Just graduated from McGill. Engaged to a psychiatrist.*

VOICE 7: *I worked for them for years. I was a waiter for thirteen summers. I must have served twenty thousand duck dinners.*

VOICE 8: *I still dream about her duck.*

VOICE 9: *And Yukle Bernstein lived over there. That's where Crystal's used to be.*

VOICE 10: *It was over there.*

VOICE 9: *No, it was there.*

VOICE 10: *You're crazy.*

VOICE 11: *We used to rent them rooms. It was a real cultural experience. I'd never met any Jewish people before.*

VOICE 12: *What were they like?*

VOICE: 11: *You know, they weren't much different than us really.*

VOICE 13: *No the synagogue is gone. They have the Founder's stone at the historical society but the building's gone.*

VOICE 14: *I can't believe it. I remember hearing them blow the* shofar *on* Rosh Hashanah.

HARRY, talking to a young MAN.

HARRY: William Shatner, he was Jewish. And Leonard Nimoy.

MAN: Mr. Spock was Jewish?

HARRY: Sure, and Red Buttons, George Burns, Kirk Douglas, Tony Curtis. Mel Tormé, Leonard Cohen, Elvis…

MAN: Elvis was Jewish?

HARRY: No, I'm pulling your leg. But Michael Jackson is.

MAN: Nooooo.

DORIS sees HARRY.

DORIS: Harry, my cousin Harry?

HARRY: Doris, is that you?

DORIS: Harry. (*She hugs him.*) I'm so glad you could come.

HARRY: Wouldn't miss it for the world.

DORIS: You look exactly the same.

HARRY: A little older, a little fatter.

DORIS: Who isn't? Tell me in twenty-five words or less. How have you been?

HARRY: Not bad.

DORIS: That's it?

HARRY: I have occasional gas.

DORIS: All right, that's enough. Can you believe it, Harry? Look at this place. Remember?

HARRY: I remember. I remember why I left it too.

DORIS: The bonfires, the weenie roasts.

HARRY: Making out in the graveyard.

Doris (Elly Ray Hennessy) reunites with her cousin Harry (Allan Price) at the Pontypool reunion.

Doris (Elly-Ray Hennessy) and Harry (Allan Price) find a treasure map.

DORIS: I didn't do that. I was a good girl. There's something special about this place. That's why all these people came back.

HARRY: I wanted to tell you. My mother, *alavashulum*, I was looking in the attic after she died and I found, it's ridiculous, but it's an old journal, of Moishe Yukle.

DORIS: You're kidding!

HARRY: I don't know how my mother ended up with it. There's not much in it to write home about, but I thought it might interest you. It's in English and Yiddish.

DORIS opens the book.

DORIS: Look at that. The Montreal Pant Factory. That's what it was called – on Maria Street.

HARRY: Ma-rye-ah.

DORIS: Whatever. Here's an order for pants. Here's an order for bolts of cloth.

HARRY: And at the back is a list of purchases in Pontypool for butter, milk, potatoes. Nothing important. Still it's from 1907 and it belonged to him. I thought you'd like to see it. It should go to the Manvers Hysterical Society.

DORIS: Historical Society. Or the Jewish archives might want it. It's an important piece of history.

Something between the pages falls to the ground.

HARRY: Something fell.

DORIS: What? (*She picks it up and opens it.*) It's a...a diagram, or a... I don't know.

HARRY: Let me see. Looks like directions.

DORIS: For what?

HARRY: Probably how to get out of Pontypool. Let's see. There's a.... there's the old homestead there, and that's where the barn was.

DORIS: There's an "X."

HARRY: Where?

DORIS: That's an "X."

HARRY: Oh, I see. So we're here.

DORIS: No we're here.

HARRY: Right; of course. So the "X is there. So, what does it mean?

DORIS: There's a number ten.

HARRY: Ten? For what, ten feet?

DORIS: If it's a treasure map, maybe it's ten steps.

HARRY: Ten steps, all right. Starting here.

DORIS: There.

HARRY: Right. Okay. *Eins, tsvey, dray, fir, finf, zeks, zibn akht, nayn, tsen.*

What do we do now?

DORIS: Dig.

HARRY: With what?

DORIS: There's a shovel over there.

HARRY: You want me to dig my grave.

DORIS: Sha! Dig a little. See if we're in the right place.

HARRY begins to dig.

HARRY: I could have a heart attack, you know. I had bypass surgery.

DORIS: I didn't know that.

HARRY: I don't like to complain. What if we hit water?

DORIS: It'll drain the pond.

HARRY: Is that thing still there? Hey. I hit something.

DORIS: What?

HARRY: My foot. No, I'm kidding, I don't know. Help me.

They pull out a metal box from the earth.

DORIS: Is it locked?

HARRY: I don't think so.

DORIS: Open it. See what it is.

They open the box.

HARRY: Oh my god.

DORIS: What is it?

HARRY pulls out a tallus and prayer book.

HARRY: It's Yukle's old whiskey still.

DORIS: No.

HARRY: Sure. Look. That's the boiler, that's where the mash goes, that's the cap arm. The thump keg. And that's the warm box.

DORIS: Oh my. So he made his own liquor.

HARRY: I told you.

DORIS: I was a kid. What did I know? What's that?

HARRY: What?

DORIS: At the bottom.

HARRY pulls out a small old-fashioned bottle with a cork on it.

HARRY: It's moonshine.

DORIS: What? You sure?

HARRY: Only one way to find out.

DORIS: What if it's poison?

HARRY: I'll die a happy man. *Baruch ata adonai, elohaynu melech ha'olam, boray pri ha goffen.* (*Blessed are you, King of the Universe, who brought forth the fruit of the vine.*)

He opens the bottle and takes a sip. He starts to cough and choke.

DORIS: Harry! Harry, you okay?

He stops coughing.

HARRY: It's delicious. Have a nip.

DORIS: I shouldn't.

HARRY: When else will you ever have hundred-year-old moonshine? Taste it.

DORIS takes a sip.

DORIS: You know, it's not bad.

HARRY takes another sip.

HARRY: That Yukle was something else. All this was because of him.

HARRY takes another drink.

DORIS: Put it away, you don't want to get drunk in the middle of the day.

HARRY: All right, but I'm taking that still home with me. It still makes perfectly good whiskey. I could start my own business.

DORIS: And go to jail.

HARRY: Better than dying in an old folks' home.

DORIS: They'll put you in with thieves and murderers.

HARRY: I worked in Toronto, what's the difference.

DORIS: You haven't changed a bit.

HARRY: A little older, a little fatter.

DORIS: You used that joke already.

HARRY: Did I? I don't remember.

DORIS: You remember what you want to remember. Come on, forget the whiskey, let's go to the Orange Hall, there's refreshments inside.

The End

An Unofficial Guide to Yiddish Words and Phrases in *The Right Road to Pontypool*

Borscht
A Russian cabbage soup. There is also a beet version but this is the cabbage version.

Bupkas
Nothing. Like what Jews get in their stockings at Christmas.

Challah
Jewish egg bread used for ceremonies and the occasional ham sandwich. (shh!)

Chupah
A tent-like awning with four poles that Jews marry under. Four poles, not Poles.

Ferkakta
Shitty. Self-explanatory.

Gefilte fish
Literally "stuffed fish," but a blend of three chopped fish, usually boiled. My family also made a fried version and it was much better, if you ask me. It's a consistency thing.

Gonuf
A thief. Like a banker or a suspicious uncle.

Ketubah
A marriage contract. They usually last longer than the marriages.

Kiddush
A ceremony of prayer and blessing over wine. Like at a *bris*, a circumcision ceremony. Because if you don't drink when someone gets their *petzl* snipped, when should you ever drink? (*Petzl*? – Ach, don't waste my time.)

Knishes
Whipped potatoes in filo pastry. Better with fried onions.

Kuchelane
A little room with a small kitchen.

Hashem
The name.

Macher
A big shot. Like the cousin who knew William Shatner when he went to Baron Byng High School.

Maideleh
A little girl. Darling. A term of endearment.

Mechia
A blessing. A relief. Like when you take your tight shoes off and it feels so good, you say "It's a mechia."

Mensch
A man. But a man who behaves like a "person." Not a man.

Meshuganahs
The crazy people. Not necessarily your family.

Mishpochas
Your family. Not necessarily crazy, but probably.

Mumzers
Bastards. The ones who charge you five cents for a plastic bag.

Nachas
Joy. Your children bring you nachas. The waitress bring you nachos.

Nisht
Nothing, zero, bupkas.

Oy
The sound a Jewish person makes when they are surprised, or in pain. Or in great pleasure. Or when they forgot to turn off the light.

Oy vay
The same sound when more lights are left on.

Pisher
A little one. A tiny penis. A small person.

Pitzikle
A little one. But not a penis. The kitten is a pitzikle. Russian, I think.

Rogalach
A delicious baked good. I like the apricot, but who can say no to chocolate?

Schmoozing
Talking with people who are important to talk to business wise. Not friends and not family. Unless you have a rich uncle.

Shiva
Sitting seven days, when a close relative dies, on low chairs with the mirrors covered and a minyan at six o'clock, with at least ten men you have never seen before, to have a prayer service.

Shmatas
Rags. The clothing business. The thing that saved the Jews in Canada.

Shmendrick
A jerk, a fool.

Shochet
A ritual slaughterer. Or as Jews would say, the butcher.

Shtetl
A Jewish village in eastern Europe. Most of them destroyed by the Nazis.

Tagalach
A pastry like *rogalach,* with more taga.

Tatala
I don't know. I think it means "dear" or "little father."

Trockele
A little truck. Whatsamatter you couldn't figure that one out?

Tuchas
You're sitting on it.

Zees
Sweet.

Zeida
Grandfather. Sometimes called Zadie. But not here.

Gay avek! Gay avek!
Go away.

Ehr iz a mumzer.
He's a bastard.

Muhn cookies.
Poppyseed cookies.

Oy oy oy a mechia.
A blessing. Jeez! How wonderful.

Sis nisht genig.
It's not enough.

Vilst epes onderish?
You want something else?

Vos ken ich teen?
What can I do?

Vus hust I gezuk?
Did you hear what I said?

Vus is a bagel?
What is a bagel?

Zei gezunt.
Bless you.

Zey zolen vaxen hoich vee bamer.
Something like – They should only grow tall like trees.